GW00481841

1

No Mama, I Didn't Die

My Life as a Stolen Baby

Devereaux R. Bruch

born Nell Howell

Dedicated to my birth mother,
Lena Mae Howell

Foreword

"Happy or unhappy, families are all mysterious."
Gloria Steinem, (1934-)

Jane Howard, author of <u>Families</u> (Simon & Schuster, 1978) was asked by Irene Neves of *PEOPLE* magazine about her findings on American families: "The family is often described as a dying institution. Is it true?"

Ms. Howard replied, "Families are changing, in flamboyant and dumbfounding ways, but the noise of these changes doesn't amount to a death knell." She continued, "Our capacity and need to be part of one family or another—perhaps of several—is one of the things that makes us human, like walking upright. If our first or second family doesn't please us, we go find ourselves a third. - There are childless couples willing to wait seven years for an adoption.

"Isn't 'blood thicker than water'? "Ms. Neves asked

"Not necessarily", Ms. Howard answered. "Our ancestors were tribal because they had no choice. But times change . . . I've seen an astonishing amount of evidence of longing for a family."As Jane Howard states in her book, "Call it a clan, call it a network, call it a tribe, call it a family. Whatever you call it, whoever you are, you need one."

Devy Bruch searched for family for the first seven decades of her life. She was stolen from her mother as an infant by the infamous Georgia Tann in 1937. She was bundled up, packaged with bows and sweet

7

smells, and sold to a wealthy Pennsylvania couple. Sadly, her adopted mother died at an early age and her adopted father, a brilliant chemist, was cold, detached, judgmental, and intolerant.

Her adoptive parents provided Devy with all the privileges that money can bring, a fine home, good schools and fine luxuries. But, there remained a longing to know more about her birth mother. Who was she? Where was she? Did she remember her baby girl? Devy kept these questions quietly to herself. It was never discussed.

Devy's path was set before her. She married young and had four children within a brief span. All seemed idyllic – until her husband declared the marriage ended and ran off with Devy's adopted brother's wife. It was a devastating time and Devy once again experienced feelings of abandonment. During this time, her adoptive father (then remarried) kept his distance and provided no emotional or financial support. Yet, Devy managed to keep the children together, hoping to create for them the sense of family she had been denied.

I met Devy in the early 1970s, after she brought her children to Florida. In the many years since, I have noted her engrained desire to create and maintain family. As Jane Howard noted, we can create family where our birth family does not exist. Devy set about establishing familiar relationships with friends and acquaintances, especially those who were alone or facing hardship.

Her doors were always open then, as they are now, to anyone in need. Food, clothing, shelter. A cup of hot tea and a warm conversation. She healed what was broken, reached to those who had, themselves, been rejected.

At times, Devy tried with near obsession to hold in-laws and stepchildren together, to blend families across the generations, to serve as mother and grandmother, aunt and friend. But, not everyone reacted favorably to these efforts. Perhaps, they had taken their own family for granted. Maybe family was no longer as important to them; their values had shifted and outlooks had changed. Maybe, they saw Devy as an interloper, reaching into their 'clan', where she didn't really belong. Devy had no clan of her own.

And now, in her 70s, Devy has finally found her family. Her real family. The roots and branches of generation after generation, those who came before her and those who came before them. Centuries of history, of belonging.

Devy had not been abandoned by her birth mother. She had been stolen. Stolen and sold. Her mother had been told that she had given birth to a baby boy, not a girl. A boy that died at birth. Lena Mae Howell went to her grave mourning the baby she had lost. And yet, as Devy would learn, Lena always suspected that her baby had lived. She remembered hearing it cry.

Perhaps, Lena Mae Howell held hope in her heart that her child was alive somewhere. And perhaps, that spirit of hope is what allowed Devy to survive all the challenges she faced in her lifetime. For, in her heart, Devy always knew she had a real family somewhere that would love her and accept her and never abandon her. This is her story.

Bill Sydnor –
author, educator and Devy's 'son' for many years

Acknowledgments

ROBIN HUNTER BUNCH, my precious daughter, who never gave up in her quest to find my origins. She put this story in my lap, with her perseverance and desire. I just needed to complete it.

PATRICIA R. WILKS, my sister who destiny denied me of for decades. Her part of this story is heart wrenching. I'm blessed to finally have her in my life.

WILLIAM SYDNOR (BILL), my editor, advisor, and surrogate son. His long hours of dedication to this endeavor brought us this story in totality. Bill is a published author in his own right of four books.

And last but not least, a very dear friend who read the final draft of my manuscript with a keen eye for approval and submission for publishing.

Let Me Begin My Story

"If a man will begin with certainties, he shall end in doubts;
but if he will be content to begin with doubts
he shall end in certainties."
Sir Francis Bacon (1561-1626)

Adoption is an honorable act, but it can be heart wrenching when the infant is surrendered under coercion or false pretenses. For the adopted parents, adoption creates instant parenthood; for the birth parents, it takes enormous courage and love to surrender a baby. Birth mothers often suffer pangs of guilt and sadness as the years tick by. They imagine how their relinquished child is faring . . .

This is my story. I am Devy Bruch, born Nell Howell in Tennessee, 1937. As an infant, I was stolen from my mother, Lena Mae Howell just eight hours after she gave birth and sold to a wealthy family through an illegal adoption in the state of Tennessee. Lena was a very young woman at the time and was told that she had given birth to a boy, who had died during delivery. My mother never saw me, nor held me. Many decades later, she went to her grave still suspecting that her baby may have survived. She had heard me cry. She knew in her heart that I could be alive, but she had nowhere to turn.

My Surrender Papers – Nell Howell

Prior to the Great Depression, from 1925 and through to 1950, Georgia Tann operated the Tennessee Children's Home Society in Memphis. She began her career by placing babies legitimately in adoptive homes in Tennessee for a fee of $7.50. Quite soon, she realized she could ship babies on a night flight with a nurse to affluent families throughout the country. She cared only about their ability to pay, not if they were suitable parents. Her fees ranged from $1,500 to $2,000 per baby, plus expenses. During this period, the average annual income in the United States was just $1,200 - $2,000.

Georgia Tann with Infant Child

Georgia Tann's modus operandi was to shelter unwed, pregnant girls or to seek out babies of the poor and promise their families good care and fine schooling. While these women were in the throes of childbirth under sedation, Georgia Tann would have them sign surrender papers. These new mothers thought they were signing permission for her to care for the baby until they could do so themselves, but they were later told their babies had died or were stillborn.

Georgia Tann was able to continue this criminal operation for decades with the protection of city officials, judges, police, etc., to whom she gave kickbacks. She accumulated great wealth, but purporting herself as 'just average', lunching daily from a paper bag at her desk.

Georgia Tann

During Georgia Tann's tenure, she placed over 5,000 babies, most illegally. Dozens of infants died in Georgia Tann's care. Many who were placed in homes experienced physical and sexual abuse. I was one of the lucky ones that survived and received a good home.

To the parents who chose to adopt me,
my heart is full of gratitude
for the wonderful life I was given.
To them, I extend my love in abundance.

And to my mother, Lena Mae,
I dedicate this story to you.
In God's time,
one day we will finally meet.

Robin's Story
– as told by my oldest daughter, Robin Hunter
Bunch

"Like a blind spinner in the sun, I tread my days:
I know that all the threads will run appointed ways."
Helen (Fiske) Hunt Jackson

From the time I was a small girl, I always wondered
about my mother's real (biological) family. I was
often told that I looked like Caroline Kennedy as a
girl. I was born the same year as Caroline. I
watched her grow through television stories and
magazines. This made my head swell with all kinds
of thoughts and dreams. You see, when you don't
have any answers about your true heritage, anything
is possible!

Let me explain why I wondered about my real roots
growing up. It started with my fear of my mother's
adoptive father, my Granddaddy. He was a difficult
man. He had no common sense and always argued
about the strangest things. I was always afraid to
talk to him for fear of saying the wrong thing and
then hearing him raise his voice. This continued
into my adulthood. He was very intimidating,
especially for a young girl to be around. He was a
brilliant man, a chemist. He was so smart, which
was why it was difficult to have a normal
conversation with him. I think his mind was always
filled with formulas and mathematical problems! He
did not know how to show emotion (except anger)
or love. He treated my mother as a hired hand on
the farm while she was growing up. Even though
she loved the farm life, she was always trying to
prove herself so her father would love her.

I admire my mother for growing up seemingly so normal and nice. To his dying day, my mother craved his love and never got it. Hearing stories while I was young and knowing my mom had been adopted made my mind wander to the most wonderful places. Was I the granddaughter of a Kennedy? Were my real relatives famous or royalty? There is no limit to a young girl's thoughts and dreams. Imagination is a wonderful thing. I often asked my mom if she ever wanted to find her real family. She always said no, she didn't want to 'open a can of worms.' Maybe she thought her real family might be worse than the father she had.

I grew up never having any answers as to my real heritage. I always knew my real Grandfather and Grandmother had to be the nicest people. No one could be like Dr. Rose, my mother's adoptive father. My mom was a nice person; she was nothing like her adoptive family with all their idiosyncrasies. Therefore, I knew my Mom could be wrong in thinking maybe her real family would be like the one she grew up with…turns out they are opposite. However, we would not know this for many, many years. We went on with our lives and we all grew up.

I again started thinking of my mom's real parents when my sister, Darryl, had her first child. We were wondering about the medical aspect of things. We, of course, had no medical history on my mother's side. I always remember those questions at the doctor's office, "Mother's medical history…. any cancer, tuberculosis, high blood pressure, etc…" I always put, "Don't know, adopted." Dawson was born and I wondered which side of the family would he look like? If it were Mom's side, we would not know whom he looked like. That was always a sad thing for me. I wondered a lot about whom we looked like and where they were. I knew I had a whole family out there somewhere. Did they know? Were they looking for us?

Daughter, Robin, and Me

Order Now for Shipping in Time for Christmas!

"There is nothing like a newborn baby to renew your spirit-"
Virginia Kelly

One cold December day, just before Christmas, a chauffeur driven limousine with a nurse and Georgia Tann delivered me to my new home. The year was 1937 and I was a sickly, five-pound weakling, six weeks of age. I had been delivered to my adoptive parents totally sight unseen, until that knock on the door - "Here is your baby."

I arrived so hungry and tiny that Mother cut the nipples off my bottles so I wouldn't have to suck so hard to get my food. Daddy noted that I had spunk. He immediately recognized that I was precocious, a trait I kept throughout my life. I had the spirit of a survivor, which would serve me well in facing the many challenges that lie ahead.

It must have been a long, arduous drive from Shelby County, Memphis, Tennessee, to this small town coal region in central Pennsylvania, where Daddy was beginning his thirty-six year career with a company then known as Atlas Powder. He was fresh out of Cal Tech, with a prior degree from Harvard. I came to know very little about his business career in the years ahead. He didn't talk about it much in front of me and my brother, six weeks my senior, who had also been adopted, but from another part of the country. I knew that Daddy was a research chemist with a doctorate degree. His work often took him overseas, where he made speeches as a part of the 'Bread Hearings', a team of four who developed the concept of preservatives for bread. I remember him going to Europe or to one of the big American cities to make a speech. Mother rarely went with him.

During the late 40's, Jonas Salk was working on a polio vaccine (I had a mild case as a young child). Atlas Chemical Industries had access to the two components needed for the vaccine, manitol and sorbitol, which were available in Egypt. Dr. Salk came to Atlas and worked with Daddy for three weeks on this project. The first charcoal filter that went into cigarettes was Daddy's invention.

His mind was superior and he seemed to know a little something about everything. He prided himself in making homemade games, puzzles and small inventions. He loved to blow glass and came up with some lovely designs in the laboratory.

My brother and I were known as the two D's, Dennis and Devereaux. For Mother and Daddy, it was like having twins and I'm sure we were a handful, especially for our housekeeper who didn't appreciate the task of potty training us. I vividly remember some of her classic language when we failed to make it to the bathroom in time and she had to clean us up. She was from Poland and had a funny, long name and a thick accent. Denny and I teased her unmercifully. I'm certain Mother often wondered if the nanny would ever live to see us grow up.

Mother was a tall, slim, attractive young woman of twenty-eight when she assumed the role of instant motherhood. Her education rivaled Daddy's, with a degree from Syracuse University, a law degree from Columbia and further studies at George Washington University. She was a refined lady, even through the years of illness that eventually took her life at the age of fifty-eight. She wanted the best for her babies and she got it.

My Brother, Dennis, and Me at One Year of Age

Very early in my life, I became keenly aware that my brother, whom I adored, had serious eye problems. Mother took him on the long train ride to Philadelphia twice a week to see the best doctors. From the time he was eighteen months old, he had to wear patches over his eyes and later wore thick glasses.

During this early period, I at times felt left out and became insecure. I felt that my brother was Mother's favorite. Daddy was busy with his career and not outwardly affectionate. The times when he bounced me on his knee and told me nursery rhymes became the special moments I cherished.

From the time Dennis and I could barely sit up, we were repeatedly read a book titled, <u>The Chosen Baby</u>. Adoption was special. We were wanted and loved and we knew it more and more as the years went past. Naturally, we rebelled against discipline, yet we learned to obey and not say bad words - the bar of Fels Naptha Soap was always nearby! Only once did I have my mouth washed out. It was a shameful experience and from then on, I knew that my parents meant what they said.

My Adoptive Mother, Janet Rose, with her Scottish Terriers

In later years, I learned Mother's weak spots, so she would bend the rules a little if I had a logical reason for wanting to do something. Daddy was stern and there were times I was afraid of him or his reactions, which were always verbal, never physical. Perhaps I was just in awe of his brilliant mind, but for years I just wanted him to come down to my level and be human, be lovable and help me with my life.

How or why did two different adoption agencies allow my parents to have two babies at once, when they lived in a tiny house in back of railroad tracks, where there was a daily accumulation of soot? As a very little girl, I posed this question to my mother. Her reply was simple, quick, to the point and I never had to wonder again. "They knew your father was going to the top." Plain and simple, n'est c'EST pas?

The road upward began shortly. Dennis and I were four years old when the family left the coal region for the thriving metropolis of Wilmington, Delaware. Atlas Powder Company gave Daddy a nice promotion and the remaining years of his career were home-based there. These were happy years for my brother and me. We went to Quaker schools, attended Meetings on Sunday and lived in a neighborhood filled with families with children. We spent part of our winters in Mount Dora, Florida, at Great Aunt Betty's estate and part of our summers at Montressor, her twelve hundred acre dairy farm in Leesburg, Virginia.

It was while visiting Aunt Betty that we learned to use finger bowls and were made to sit through two-hour dinners while the butler served us each course. Our most proper manners were always present. Perfecting my curtsey would come in very handy later on, during debutante season in Philadelphia. Great Aunt Betty lived all alone, and I felt her life must have been sad and lonely. I had heard that her husband, the grandson of the founder of one of the country's largest steel companies, had been placed away in a sanatorium years before. And he died there. I have thought of Aunt Betty so often through the years. She brought such joy into my young life.

As the years passed, I realized that there was usually a reason for everything Mother and Daddy did. We learned their lessons from experience, even though I thought many were unfair at the time. My parents taught us to be able to stand alone, to save our money, to survive in a tough world. Today, I am deeply grateful to them for those lessons. Dennis and I are now adults, with grown children of our own. For me, the heritage my mother gave me was one of fineness, goodness, love of mankind and humility. I am grateful that I was able to tell her of my love and appreciation for adopting me and shall always cherish her memory.

My father, who is in part the inspiration for my writing, taught me to have goals and follow through with them, to have sensible values, and to love animals. Most importantly, he taught me that "life is tough, kid . . . face it and deal with it straight on."

Me on My "Daddy's" Knee

My Early Days in the Coal Regions

"And hie him home, at evening's close,
To sweet repast and calm repose."
Thomas Gray

We soon moved from our first floor apartment, which had railroad tracks in back. So much soot accumulated from the trains that I asked Mother how in the world she and Father were allowed to adopt two babies living where we did. Mother replied, "They knew your father was on his way up."

Our new home, the Blakey House was a white clapboard with a white picket fence around it. Here I had such happy memories. Once a week, after work, Daddy would take me to the Firehouse, sit me on the bar and drink beer with his buddies and they'd be so nice to me. I had a friend who lived in the woods behind us and we'd play dolls and dress up her puppy in doll clothes.

At Christmas, Dennis and I snuck out of bed on Christmas Eve. Sitting at the top of our winding staircase, we saw our parents stuffing stockings and putting out toys. We were sure Santa had gotten sick and was unable to reach our house.

During the War, we had blackouts. When the sirens sounded, black shades went down on all the windows and lights went out. Tamaqua, PA, for a short interlude, became totally blacked out. I thought it all very exciting.

29

At 5 years old, I didn't want to leave my happy existence to move to Delaware, but it was inevitable. Daddy had received a big promotion – Director of Research.

My Brother, Dennis, and Me at Age Three

Dennis and Me at Age Four

Adventures – a New Home in a New State

"The great thing in this world is not so much where you stand,
as in what direction you are moving."
Oliver Wendell Holmes (1809-1894)

I adapted well to our new home, but poor Dennis was still having serious eye problems. Mother took him to Philadelphia on the train every week to an eye specialist. He had to wear black patches on his eyes and later, very thick glasses. During this time, I felt that my brother was the favored child, but I grew out of those emotions as I matured. Denny was the cutest boy, a blonde towhead, but more introverted than I.

We moved to a lovely flagstone house in a quiet neighborhood with many children close to our age. There were woods in the back, with a stream and big rocks to climb on. This was a wonderful venue for hide 'n seek; we could go through the woods to visit our friends. I couldn't wait to get home from school so that I could play jacks with my pal, Sara. We became champions and could out-play almost anyone. I was in the same class as Sara at a very nice Quaker school in Wilmington. Having been baptized an Episcopalian in the National Cathedral in Washington, D. C., I had an excellent background for membership in the Religious Society of Friends, known to many as the Quakers.

Here I am at Age Six with Dennis

Daddy thought we needed a truck garden to grow our own vegetables and a good part of our education went toward fostering this endeavor. I adored watching things grow and learning to care for them. About this time, Mother thought I needed a little kitten to raise, nurture and care for. "Dumpling" appeared one afternoon upon my return home from school. Oh, what a darling little thing! I cared for her as if she were my own baby. It was the start of my love for all living things and my instinct to nurture. It was the start of my need to create and maintain a sense of family.

Extended Family Matters

"Smile at each other, make time for each other in your family."
Mother Teresa (1910-1997), *in her Nobel lecture*

Daddy had an Aunt (his mother's sister) who was Victorian and looked the part. She maintained a thousand acre dairy farm in Leesburg, Virginia and a lake house in Mount Dora, in central Florida. She had a huge dining room table and a butler who wore white gloves. When I was a child, we had to sit at the table for very long dinners, just our family and Aunt Betty.

She had no children and lived alone. We were told that her husband had gone mad and was committed to a sanatorium. Her husband was Page Laughlin, the grandson of the founder of Jones and Laughlin Steel Co. in the Pittsburgh area. Perhaps today, with modern medicine and diagnostic techniques, he would have been diagnosed with Alzheimer's disease and been allowed to live a more normal life.

Aunt Betty was very kind and good to us. She taught me how to curtsey, which stood me in good stead later in life during my debutante year. Driving to Mt. Dora in Florida each year must have been a chore for Mother. Daddy stayed home part of the time to work. Of course, our car had no seat belts then. En route, I was playing with the door handle on the passenger side of the front seat when the door swung open and I began to fall out of the moving car! Mother grabbed my dress and came to a stop. She must have been frantic!

33

Aunt Betty died in 1948. I recall hearing that she left us a substantial amount of money and enough antiques and oriental rugs to furnish our next venture.

Dear Aunt Betty and Me at Montressor

The Two "D"s – Devereaux and Dennis – at age Three
on Aunt Betty's Farm

In Mount Dora, Florida, with the Draper Cousins-
I am on the Far Left and Dennis (wearing glasses)
is on the Far Right

Linden Farm

"When tillage begins, other arts follow —
The farmers therefore are the founders of human civilization."
Daniel Webster

By 1948, unbeknownst to Daddy, Mother was becoming restless. She was spending her days with a realtor, exploring the wide-open spaces just over the Pennsylvania state line. She found her utopia: 109 acres of rolling country with a main house, a carriage house, a huge barn with a tack house, pig pens, chicken coops, a grape vineyard and an apple orchard. Daddy was totally overwhelmed by it all. Mother usually got her way and she was determined to live in historic Revolutionary War country. I knew my cat Dumpling would love her new home, far away from the main roads.

So, at the close of the school year, we moved to Linden Farm, down the road from Chadd's Ford. This move began an incredible adventure for Dennis and me. It expanded our knowledge in so many ways and was truly character building.

The first thing we did was run through the house. There were so many rooms, with huge marble fireplaces in most of them and so many winding staircases that we got lost. The cellar alone had nine rooms and two big ovens in the stone wall. We learned that the house, built in 1724, was an inn during the Revolutionary War and that the Battle of the Brandywine started on the property.

Linden Farm

There were cannons and commemorative plaques in several locations around the property and a hole in the kitchen wall, which was a porch at the time, made by a cannon ball during the battle. The British, who were advancing from Valley Forge, had fired that cannon ball into the porch. The battle began on September 11, 1777. General George Washington summoned the Marquis de Lafayette to come from France to help plot the battle. They lunched together several times in this house, in the room to the right of the vestibule, later known as the Lafayette Room.

Everything in the house was original: cabinets, floors with boards so wide and solid, even the wine cellar under the main cellar. We learned that our house was once a stop on the Underground

Railroad. That sparked the next adventure for Dennis and me.

Believing there was an actual railroad under the house, and the floor in the wine cellar being dirt, we began digging. We became frustrated at only finding old pounds of lard and a few Queen Victoria coins, which we sold to a neighbor-boy for a quarter. Mom and Dad felt it time to tell us the history of the "underground railroad," and what had really happened and that the name was just a figure of speech. There were many houses like ours that harbored escaped slaves by day, moving them North by night, helping to get them safely out of the South. Our house was perfect for hiding the slaves, with its huge basement and ovens for baking. This was all terribly exciting for Dennis and me.

Artist's Rendering of Linden Farm

Linden Farm was named for the huge Linden trees (four of them) that surrounded the front entrance of the house. They were about 250 years old, as the local historian, Chris Sanderson, told us. Chris operated a little museum in Chadds Ford. He was the local fiddler and for generations taught every child in the county to square dance. He knew the history of Chester County better than anyone. He made a point of showing up at several of the historic homes on Chester County Day when the homes were open to the public, to make sure the guides were giving accurate information. Denny and I were 13 when Mother decided to open our home to the public. Chris Sanderson stood with me in the entry hall for most of the day, teaching me the facts and how to be a docent. I loved it. Speaking in front of a crowd gave me self-esteem and confidence. In point of fact, I was something of a ham and I became more self-assured with each of the three years the house was open.

We would have more than 1,400 people go through the house each Chester County Day, always the first Saturday of October.

Daddy threw himself into contour farming, cattle raising, sheep shearing, and cow milking, actually raising most of our food. We churned our own butter and reached under the hens for our daily fresh eggs. By day, Daddy was a research chemist at Atlas, in Wilmington, Delaware, but he couldn't wait to get home to bring in the hay, help deliver a calf, collect eggs, feed pigs, and boil water for fresh corn. He loved it. His big workshop in the carriage house was where he made our toys and puzzles. There was also a large incubator and pen for the baby peeps (chicks). Each April, we'd get 100 at a time. It was fun watching them grow and seeing which ones were the girls and which ones were the boys. The males had huge combs on their heads and bright coloring. The females had little combs and lighter coloring. We usually got New Hampshire Reds; they laid large, brown eggs.

A year after we took up residence at the farm, Mother felt it time for me to have a horse. Two were for sale at a neighboring farm where they had a big riding ring. I could have lessons there and then decide which horse was best for me. I picked a roan colored horse, probably 16 hands high and named him Cinnamon Bun. He became my pal, my confidante and my best friend. I fed him fresh carrots from the garden, apples from the orchard and sugar cubes from the kitchen. I brushed him religiously and rode him almost daily. His stall was next to our two milk cows where he could see me and the many barn cats that would come around at milking time. I would always squirt warm milk into their mouths. I was raised on raw milk and the cream that floated to the top so rich it was churned into our butter.

I know that all the fresh foods grown on the farm contributed to my good health as I grew up. The cows and steers were tested periodically for TB and bangs, diseases that farm animals can incubate. We usually had 2 bulls and 10 heifers, with 10 calves born annually. In the beginning we raised Guernsey's, but after a few years, we switched to Black Angus. Daddy said the meat had a better flavor. Neighbors and friends clamored to be on the list to get ½ a steer, butchered to their specifications. The same happened with the sheep and the pigs.

I learned to love exotic breakfasts such as pickled tongue, kidneys wrapped in bacon and broiled, sweetbreads and chicken livers sautéed in butter and served on toast. Breakfast was always the most important meal each day. The hens, on the other hand, were quite intimidating and pecked the daylights out of my arms and hands as I reached under them to remove the warm, fresh eggs. I learned to wear heavy gloves when collecting eggs.

As chickens are cannibalistic, I took great pains to save a very sick hen being unmercifully pecked to death by other chickens. First, I got a bushel basket from the barn and put a lot of fresh straw in it. Denny helped me lift the hen into the basket and then we got her into the kitchen, next to a radiator to keep her warm. She had a pool of blood on her back. I nursed her wounds, gave her water and hand-fed her cracked corn from the corncrib in the barn. I stayed up with her all night that first night and soon she began to rally. This was a great lesson in love and sacrifice and I did learn to love that chicken. Each day she became stronger and seemed to know that I was helping her and that she was safe. Eventually, she was ready to spread her wings and would sit on my shoulder like a parrot. Daddy and I created a special pen for her next to the big chicken pen. She was among her own, yet safe from harm. She was so tame that when I'd come home from school, she was happy to see me.

During our early years on the farm, I was taught how to artificially inseminate cows and nurture newborn piglets. 'Ole Suey', mama pig, had 12 spigots (nipples) and usually delivered 13 piglets. That meant that one was the runt of the litter and needed special handling. So, the bushel basket and straw came in handy again, now to nurture and bottle-feed a baby pig. That was the most fun for me and he took to the bottle ravenously. I would hold him like a real baby while he nursed. Eventually, it was time to return him to his mother and siblings. He was still incredibly tame and always ran over to see me whenever I was within sight.

Dennis loved other things more, so usually retreated to his room to devour every book he could. His eyes had become so much better through the years, due to proper care and private tutoring for reading. He was making up for lost time and became the best-read person I have ever encountered. I was mischievous, curious and wanted to know everything I could about this wonderful environment. My father and I shared my happiest moments there and I wasn't afraid of him anymore. We did everything together; Daddy relied on me and I loved him for it.

I never liked it when busloads of school children came up the driveway to go through the house because of its historical significance, but I got used to it – and had to explain why there was a cannon ball hole in the kitchen wall!

Once a year the drapes came down and everything was specially cleaned in anticipation of Chester County Day, always the first Saturday in October. This was when the public was permitted to go through the historic homes in the area. As I grew older, I truly appreciated the full extent of what this day meant to Mother and the pride she felt. The farm was her baby and we all loved it with her. Years later, she was laid to rest atop a hill overlooking her domain.

Country Life

*"The Leaves fall, the wind blows, and the farm country slowly
changes from the summer cottons into its winter wools."*
Henry Beston

Every Saturday morning, one of the local hunts
would ride over our fields with perhaps three-dozen
foxhounds in tow, chasing the fox. The riders were
dressed in full regalia with bright red jackets,
ascots, jodhpurs, tall boots and black derby hats. It
was a picture worth painting. The fox was grey, not
red, but it was illegal to kill a fox in Pennsylvania.
As the dogs would corner the fox, the Master of the
Hounds would blow his horn, signaling the dogs to
stop on a dime. They were magnificently trained
and it was great sport.

After the hunt, breakfasts were held at one of the
local farmhouses, usually a lavish spread and
wonderful camaraderie. Periodically after a
steeplechase or horse show, the horsy crowd
gathered for more formal parties at various Hunt
Clubs in the area. It was at one of these parties, at
age 15, that I had my first cocktail -a daiquiri. I felt
very grown up and probably was more mature than
most girls my age due to all the responsibility I had
assumed on the farm from the age of 8. My first
beau was 18 and he's the one who gave me that
daiquiri. He was a freshman at Penn State, studying
architecture.

Father Divine's 'Angels', Something Askew!

". . . desire - in excess caused the angels to fall – "
Sir Francis Bacon

Mother was seeking out full time, live-in help. She wasn't happy during hay season when Daddy, our hired-man (who lived above the carriage house) and I didn't come in for dinner 'til dark, long after dinner was ready. It was important to get the hay in the barn before rain could ruin it. Wet hay causes combustion and can set a barn on fire. I always drove the 1929 Model A Ford truck or the 1930 Farmall tractor with the big hay wagon hooked to the rear. These were such happy times for me.

In Gladwyne, Pennsylvania, about a forty-minute drive from the farm, Mother discovered a religious sect. The leader was known as Father Divine and his followers were called "angels," all with very interesting names. "Trustworthy" came to live with us and stayed in quarters over the kitchen, a large bedroom, bathroom and a small study. She could come down a winding staircase and directly into the kitchen, without going near the rest of the house.

"Trusty", as we called her, seemed to have a man-friend who would sneak into the house without anyone's knowledge. A few months later, "Trusty" was gone and Mother told me later that she was pregnant. So much for Father Divine and his "angels"!

47

Growing Up on the Farm

"An unlesson'd girl, unschool'd, unpractised;
Happy in this, she is not yet so old; But she may learn."
Shakespeare

I spread my wings in all directions while growing up at Linden Farm. Everything that I am today was nurtured and developed there. My insatiable quest for knowledge sometimes got me in trouble. After all, Mr. Bull was my friend and I loved jumping over the pasture fence after school and sitting by the big salt block. Mr. Bull was licking away as I sang to him and our conversations ran the gamut. He looked at me and shook his head, returning to the salt with his huge tongue. Daddy had forbidden me to go near Mr. Bull. "He will butt you with his horns and will hurt you. Stay out of the pasture, Devereaux, that's final." He always called me by my full name when he was serious with his discipline. However, I spent so much time talking to Mr. Bull from over the fence that I felt safe. I knew I shouldn't wear red or bright colors and run in the pasture, egging him on to chase me. Gradually, I knew he understood my calm voice and I could just tell by the look on his face that he was my friend. Months later, when "bull sessions" were discovered, it was not a good day.

I discovered the wild things that grew on the farm, such as wine berries, similar in color and taste to a raspberry. Daddy and I would spend hours picking them and making the best darn jelly. Then the two cherry trees by the back porch yielded so much fruit that we made cherry pies 'til the cows came home.

I'd spend hours taking the stones out and learning from Daddy how to make delicious pies from scratch.

Daddy was the better cook and always insisted that one needs to only buy staples such as sugar, flour, shortening and make things from scratch. He learned his love for food preparation as a small boy from Annie, his family's cook, who stayed with the Rose family for fifty years in Marquette, MI where Daddy was raised.

The barn was a haven for wild cats and we had our share. Mother decided to buy Puss'n Boots cat food by the case and I began feeding them in the wood shed, out the side door off the kitchen. Twice a day, at least 22 cats of all ages and sizes would show up for their plates of food and fresh milk from our two milking cows. The kittens were so dear to me. I raised them all and made sure each got a fair share of the food. My "Dumpling" was basically an indoor cat, yet she got out on occasion. How could I have known that she'd get pregnant? I was too young to know about those things. One day, when I came home from school, I couldn't find my Dumpling. Mother was busy entertaining friends for lunch. I ran all over the house searching for Dumpling. Mother said she might have found a quiet place to have her babies.

I found her in the basement in the coal bin, struggling to expel a kitten that appeared lifeless. Three little ones were already born, but she was in trouble. What to do? I ran upstairs and told the ladies what was happening. One took a white hankie embroidered with lace from her purse and told me to gently pull the kitten out, holding its head with the hankie. For a little girl of ten, this was an historic event for me. Dumpling looked at me with eyes of love, knowing that I was helping her. She breathed a sigh of relief as the kitten was expelled. My mission now was to get her and the remaining three babies out of the coal bin into a cozy warm basket of straw. Dennis was always great at helping me with these missions of mercy. I felt so good, seeing Dumpling relaxed and comfortable. I prepared a warm bowl of fresh milk with a little baby cereal in it. That would give her the nourishment she needed to feed her kittens. They thrived and I watched them grow into precious little playmates. It amazed me that baby cats open their eyes for the first time at 10 days old, without fail. The gestation period is always 63 days for cats and dogs. Most of my life I have marveled that these animals can develop such superior senses and cleverness in just two months, from mating to birth.

Above the woodshed, where I fed the kittens, was a large smokehouse. It was here that we smoked hams and other meats. We had a couple of huge brown crocks that held our fresh grated cabbages in brine that Daddy made. In 2-3 weeks, we had the best sauerkraut, with plenty to give away.

Adolescence for the Two 'D's

"When you're a teenager and you're in love,
it's obvious to everyone but you -"
John Scalzi

It was not unusual for Denny and me to have our class come to the farm on weekends. As we entered puberty, we had crushes on the opposite sex, most of whom wore braces on their teeth. Parties at Linden Farm became very popular. Dennis and I prided ourselves in making tunnels in the barn with straw bales. We were the only ones who knew where the tunnels led. It was our secret. Mother loved these class parties and did a bang-up job preparing for them.

She had a favorite caterer in Wilmington, Hanna's. They would come and put umbrella tables around the pool chairs and supply a lovely spread of food. Most of the class was running through the barn and organizing kissing games, such as "spin the bottle." It was not unusual for a few kids to get in the tunnels and smooch away. One couple didn't surface for a couple hours. A boy whom I didn't like much - he had grabby hands - cornered me in one of the tunnels and tried to kiss me. I was able to get my shoe off and hit him over the head. He was quite mad at me for some time, probably from hurt feelings.

Of course there was lots of swimming and on occasion Daddy would hook up the hay wagon to the old Farmall tractor, put lots of hay and a couple pitch forks in it and load us up for a hayride to the local pub, The Farmer in the Dell. It was about a three-mile ride down the winding back road. Mother used to say the road was laid out by a drunk during The Revolutionary War. Oh, the fun we had, riding parallel to the Brandywine River, past Andrew Wyeth's (America's foremost painter) home. In the wintertime, the Brandywine froze over and we had wonderful ice-skating parties and toasted marshmallows in a fire pit. The Farmer in the Dell was the most quaint, fun place. Daddy knew the owner well and he always had a special room for all of us.

Beer was served in pitchers and a chef would carve a huge "Steamship Round of Beef" for sandwiches. There were peanut shells on the floor, pinball machines to play and dart games. Most of us had no T. V. or the tech toys and certainly no cell phones. It was a wonderful time to grow up; we made our own fun and were better off because of it.

Life's Lessons, Learned First Hand

"It is a denial of justice
not to stretch out a helping hand to the faller;
that is the common right of humanity"
Seneca (5 BC- 65 AD)

Mother and Father had sent me to The Boston School of Cookery and upon my return to the farm an event occurred that touched me deeply to this day. Mother became aware of a family with eleven children, one with a cleft palate, who had taken up residence in a barn just a short distance from our farm. Mama rallied the troops at neighboring farms to help this family who were in dire straits. Food, blankets, clothes . . . everything was rounded up and a job was found for the father of this brood.

Shelter was eventually found through the Quakers. I rode my horse down to see how they were doing several times and to drop off a few things. The smiles, love and gratitude on their faces was heart wrenching. People helping people in need; isn't that what love and compassion are all about? I do wonder at times, where did I get this nurturing instinct? Real happiness is the joy we find in doing for others; it's so easy.

A Wedding in the Country, Complete with Farm Animals

"A successful marriage is an edifice

that must be rebuilt every day."

Andre Maurois (1885-1967)

I was married on the farm on September 11th, 1956 in the Music Room, across the vestibule from the Lafayette Room. I felt like a princess coming down the winding staircase in a bone colored, Alencon lace gown with beautiful Rosepoint lace veil, Mantia style. Mother had purchased the Rosepoint lace in France a few years earlier and knew just what it would be for one day.

Dinner was served after the ceremony on the huge terraces out back, overlooking the pool and the pasture with strolling musicians adding to the charm of the evening. The cattle seemed to enjoy it too, as they all lined up at the fence to observe. Naturally, the dogs and cats mingled with the guests, hoping for droppings from everyone's plates. It was a happy time full of special memories to cherish.

My new husband and I left for Atlantic City after dark. Mother had bought me a Mollie Parnis soft jersey dress with matching hat. I felt so well put together. The Traymore Hotel expected our arrival. Flowers and champagne were nicely displayed in the bridal suite.

My new father-in-law, whom I loved dearly, had the insurance on most all of the big hotels in Atlantic City, so I'm sure we received special treatment.

Graduation Day – Agnes Irwin School – June 12, 1955

Years of Despair

"I have sometimes been wildly, despairingly,
acutely miserable, racked with sorrow,
but through it all I still know quite certainly
that just to be alive is a grand thing."

Agatha Christie (1890-1976)

After 17 years of marriage and four children, I was demoted to a second-class citizen. The grass must have appeared greener on the other side - my husband abandoned us for new horizons. The impact on four young children would be monumental for many years to come. They could never fully understand how he could leave us completely with no Christmas gifts, no birthday cards. It was total abandonment.

What was I to do? I was left with no money, all the bills which needed attention and I no visible means of support? Mother had died in 1967 and Daddy then remarried an old-maid schoolteacher who did not believe in family and kept Daddy all to herself.

They left for Florida shortly after their 1972 marriage. Daddy cried as he gave up his beloved farm, watched his cattle go to auction and the magnificent antiques and oriental rugs end up for sale at a public auction. I was not offered one thing I had grown up with because Daddy let her run the show and did not want to create any waves. I went to the auction to buy the antique sleigh bed I was raised in. It was a popular item and the bidding started high. Fortunately, the auctioneer was a friend of mine from school days; he knew my dilemma, so he cut the bidding off abruptly as I bid $500. "Sold!" he exclaimed. I have enjoyed that beautiful bed through the years, even though some feel it is haunted and will not sleep in it when they visit.

There we were, totally alone up on the hill from Linden Farm in the beautiful home my husband and I built in Daddy's upper alfalfa field just three years before. My husband was completely gone and the four children and I were quite far out in the country.

For quite some time, no one knew that he had abandoned us. Through children at school, my dilemma suddenly surfaced. For during the night, bushel baskets of produce appeared on the front door step, from their parents' gardens and orchards. There was a bounty of fresh vegetables and fruits, fresh eggs, all given to us anonymously. I knew the Quakers had opened their hearts -it was all from them.

We lived next to Birmingham Quaker Meeting House and Mother was buried in the cemetery adjoining the meetinghouse. I had taught first day school there and led the singing at Sunday Meetings for some time.

The Octagonal Schoolhouse
Where I Taught Sunday School

There was no alimony in Pennsylvania and child support was difficult to get. My husband left the state and chose to send support sporadically or not at all. My children were 16, 14 and 12 year-old twins, two boys and two girls. I knew I was the only person my children could count on and many nights I cried myself to sleep wondering how we'd make it. The children told me years later that they had heard me crying in my bedroom and they were very sad.

With no visible means of support, my immediate goal was to develop a game plan to care for my children the best way I could. I sat them down and told them the truth - that our situation was grave and I had not been trained for a career outside the home. I needed to go to work, at anything I could find, and at their young ages they would need to take on responsibility.

**Here I am With My Brood –
Dirk, Brooke, Darryl and Robin**

We needed to be a team and help each other. It tore
me apart to leave them alone at night when I went
to work in a local restaurant, a high-end inn during
the Revolutionary War, the quaint Chadds Ford Inn.
The dining rooms were small with original, wide
wooden floorboards. The bar was small too,
perhaps 10 stools, with four small round tables on
the opposite side. The local gentry and
accomplished artists dined there often and the gang
gathered at the bar each day after work.

Dorothy Theodore was the owner of the Chadds
Ford Inn and she greeted her dining guests
graciously as she seated them. My husband and I
had dined there often. Now, I was on the other side

of the fence, in uniform as a waitress. Dorothy befriended me, probably feeling a bit sorry for me. I never let her down. I learned my lessons well; the first night I brought home $72 in tips and dropped it on the kitchen counter. It was 2 in the morning when I finally fell into bed. The first child to awake the next morning ran into my room, "Mom, where did all that money come from?" I told him that as a soon as I could we'd get food in house. It was a good day, but I was tired.

The Historic Chadds Ford Inn,
Chadds Ford, Pennsylvania

Rudy was the big chef at the "Inn" and had been there for years. He saved me all the good leftovers. I'd make pots of soup or stew for the children and was ever so grateful to Rudy for his kindnesses.

When I moved to Florida, I gave Rudy all my husband's clothes that he left behind. Rudy especially liked the Chesterfield coat. I learned a good lesson that I now share with other young mothers - make friends with owners of restaurants. So much food is thrown away - why not ask them to give it to you?

Another tip - buy powdered milk. It was then only eight cents a quart. I'd mix it with water, chill it, then put a bit of chocolate syrup or Ovaltine in it. Alas, the kids never knew the difference and the nourishment was the same.

Minute Rice Anyone?

*"The ability to delude yourself
may be an important survival tool."*
Jane Wagner

A good breakfast each morning is essential for growing children; they function better in school and have more energy to perform daily tasks. Everything that goes down our throats affects our health, from our hair to our teeth and the development of all our body functions, organs and bones. I didn't want my children to see me retching over the kitchen sink from the stress and despair but one morning it was inevitable. We had killed off and eaten the chickens and the garden was completely bare. My life was in turmoil and I wondered if I would live through it. I still had a long way to go. The children were teenagers and needed my guidance, nurturing and love to show them the way.

My son Dirk was the first to come down that morning for breakfast. He put his hand on my shoulder and asked, "Why are you crying Mom?" "The cupboards are bare, my son. I have nothing to give you for breakfast except a box of minute rice." His demeanor was strong for a 12-year old lad. He was going to cheer me up, or else. "Mom, Sister, we're studying about China in school and did you know that rice is their main staple? They eat a bowl of it everyday." With that, he took a pot from the cupboard, put water and a touch of salt in the water, carefully measured out the rice, and followed the directions.

As each child came to the kitchen for breakfast, he excitedly told them that they were having a Chinese breakfast and that his teacher would be pleased that he prepared this meal for us. Before he left to catch the school bus at the end of the driveway, he said, "Now Mom, I'll be a little late after school. I'm going to stop in to see the guy (caretaker) that runs the cemetery next door to see if he'll give me a job on weekends mowing the grass around the tombstones. I'll bet I can get that job, then I'll give you the money for food."

This event and the strength of character it showed in one so young changed my life in a very positive way. Yes, he got the job in the cemetery and earned $16 each weekend. He gave me every cent for food. About this time in his life, he was developing a keen interest in archery. He began hunting rabbits in the huge woods behind our house. Before long, I'd open the door to the garage and see a rabbit hanging from the rafters. Rabbit stew became a part of our lives, thanks to Dirk's skills.

Soon, I began working at Hank's Place, the local morning eatery for locals and truckers. I left with the children each morning, and was home when they got home from school.
I was the sandwich specialist and the owners gave me great leeway to please the patrons. There were only 12 stools at the counter, no tables. It was a very tiny place.

Hank's Place, a Local Eatery in Chadds Ford

There were times when patrons stood four deep in back of the stools. I always enjoyed it when Andrew and Betsy Wyeth came in for a hot dog smothered with onion and mustard relish, which we fresh daily. Andrew was our local artist of great renown and we locals protected their privacy at all times.

I knew that I couldn't keep our beautiful home on four acres of Daddy's hayfield. There was no home in the area that I could afford and I had no credit as a divorcee, with barely enough income to feed my children.

Florida – Sun, Sand, Survival

*"Vitality shows not only in the ability to persist,
but the ability to start over."*
F. Scott Fitzgerald (1896-1940)

In my 35th year, I had monumental decisions to make. Remaining in Chester County, PA was no longer an option. I had no visible means of support and very meager funds. My ex-husband's mother lived in Fort Lauderdale and the bond of friendship remained exceptionally strong until her death many years later. She wanted us to come and take an apartment in her building on the beach so she could be close to the children.

My father and his second wife lived only twenty minutes away in Pompano Beach, Florida, but they proved to be no help to us at all. I saw a weakness in Daddy's character that crushed me. We had once been so close while we were doing chores together on the farm, all through my years growing up. His new wife now wore the pants and wanted Daddy all to herself. I think she felt that since I was adopted, I wasn't Daddy's real child. She made comments to that effect on many occasions. In any case, she had him and he wasn't allowed to see me for years. I was abandoned again.

Preparing to get us all to Florida was a Herculean task. I couldn't take my precious animals and they had to be tended to. Three of my children flew down ahead of me to stay with Mahie (Grandma) who got them settled into her apartment. I packed up the station wagon, Beverly Hillbillies style, and one of the boys drove with me. We arrived at our 2-bedroom apartment in the late summer of 1974, just in time to register for the children for school.

The schools in South Florida were a disappointment to me. The public school system in Florida in the 1970's seemed inferior to the schools in Pennsylvania. The classrooms were open; there were no walls between classrooms, which I felt was not conducive to learning. It didn't take long to realize that my children were bored. They had already learned the curriculum they were being given. With no funds for a pricey private school, we just had to float along and do the best we could.

A Most Unusual Job

"Because I am a woman, I must make unusual efforts to succeed-no one will say, 'She doesn't have what it takes'."
Clare Booth Luce *(1903-1987)*

I was a woman of 35 with no visible means of support, no college degree and four children to support with no help from an ex-husband or father. Who on earth would hire me?

Well, wonders never cease. My trump card was my loving mother-in-law, who seemed to have friends in high places. A cocktail party was organized for me to meet some very nice people. One lady asked me a lot of questions about what I knew about Medieval History. I told her that the lavish banquets during the Renaissance period intrigued me.

"Why did the men need to prove their prowess by tossing their food and bones over their shoulders for the little ladies in waiting to pick up?" I asked. That struck a chord with her.

"Gracious," she explained "I have a very dear friend who owns a beautiful Olde English restaurant here in town and he wants to bring a dinner theatre show to his restaurant with a Medieval Banquet theme. He's looking for someone to be his Director of Sales and organize the entertainers, help pick the costumes and perhaps sing a little." I was in awe as to what was about to happen to me. I needed to go to work. A restaurant would provide me a free meal perhaps. I jumped into the frying pan, full blaze!

71

The next day, I lunched with the owner of the restaurant. It would be a massive undertaking and I was a bit frightened. I knew I could sing. After all, Mother had given me piano and voice lessons early on. It would be great for my self-esteem, as I was still shattered by my very bitter divorce. I would get the chance to meet lots of new people.

Together, the owner and I hired a publicity firm, made brochures, bought space on two billboards, and booked many speaking engagements where I could introduce this venture to the public.

A wonderful, flamboyant producer had been hired. He was in charge of the hiring of entertainers, all 23 of them. We had very professional people: two Double Mint twins for court jesters, a King and a Queen, and pinchable wenches. There was a strolling banjo player and monks who carried the whole roasted pig and elaborate menu around the room on gold litters. All 200 guests enjoyed overflowing mugs of wine, poured by the wenches, who sat on the laps of the gents while pouring their libations.

I was Maid Marion, dressed in a hooped skirt with train and matching dunce-type tall hat with tulle cascading to the waist. I checked everyone in, welcomed them with a curtsey, and then joined the show with my falsetto soprano voice. At the end of the show, while most of the entertainers greeted the guests, I passed out their checks. Oh yes, I did the payroll, too.

My boss, the owner of the restaurant, was happy with my performance. Soon, I became the mascot for the Fort Lauderdale Rotary Club, greeting them each Tuesday at lunch and helping to serve them promptly. They often invited me to their special events, especially when they were going offshore on their boats. I would serve drinks and food and would organize their agenda.

These were very happy times for me. Medieval Banquets were also good to my children, who ate for free anytime they came when I was working - usually each night for dinner. Fortunately, the restaurant was within walking distance of our apartment, another bonus that was important to me.

Ties That Bind – Or Worse!

"Threats don't work with a person who has nothing to lose."
Maduro Ash

Our endeavor into Medieval History lasted a bit more than a year. I began to hear rumblings that the restaurant might be sold. On occasion, I'd seen tough looking men surveying the place. One day, the head chef, whom we all adored (he'd fix us anything to eat), asked to speak to me. He told me that he was quite certain that the Syndicate (a/k/a Mafia) was buying the restaurant. Very shortly thereafter, one of those men came up to me and asked me if I was happy with my job.

"Oh, yes," says I.

"If this restaurant is sold and you want to leave, speak to me first," he uttered. About this time, I was feeling a little betrayed. Why wasn't the owner talking to me directly? Was it because I rebuffed his romantic advances? I was sure of it. After all, he was married and I would never do to someone else's family what had been done to mine.

I was afraid of the Mafia, yet I knew I had to arrange one last party before I took off like a bandit. I just knew it was Mafia-run - a wedding at 2 a. m. that kept me up all night. It was my last hurrah there. The tips were great. Never had I seen so many hundred-dollar bills floating around; I was the recipient of three of them that last night. It was the most money I had ever had in my hand at once.

Is There a Doctor in the House?

"Overcoming the challenges makes life worth living."
Mary Tyler Moore

I found it increasingly more difficult to leave my children alone so much, yet I had to work to pay the bills. Adolescents left alone for any period of time can and will get into trouble. I always wanted to be a stay-at-home mom, but I fully understand the extenuating circumstances that drive women with children into the job market. It is a path I never intended to travel.

The employees in my apartment building seemed to know I had a tough road; I was treated with great respect. The day my son and his friend smoked pot then got on the roof of our high-rise building and began throwing large stones into the parking lot, denting six cars, was a horror for me. I had visions of being sued and thrown out on the street. When I returned from work and entered the lobby, the doorman greeted me with grace and politeness as he always did. Then he dropped this tale of woe on my shoulders. How could I continue to cope with these responsibilities? They seemed insurmountable. I put lists on the refrigerator for the children to do each morning before I went to work. Each day, the lists went ignored. At the time, good friends flew down from Pennsylvania and took my rock-throwing son back with them for a year of a stricter environment. It was a blessing and gave me some breathing room.

In times like these, it would have been good to have my mother, Lena Mae, in my life I am sure she and my sister, Pat would have been there for the children and me. My dear adopted mother had died when I was just 30 years old and my mother-in-law was now in her late 80s, so I tried not to trouble her with my worries. I was left totally alone with the raising of my children. Their father, who had abandoned them, continued to have little or no contact with us. One day, my boys got into a serious fight when I was at work and a sharp conch shell came between them. I got a call from the emergency room of local hospital that one of my sons had serious cuts over much of his body, and required nearly 100 stitches to close his wounds. I had no medical insurance. A call to the children's father, who lived only 40 minutes away, brought this response,

"Devy, you have custody of the children - - you take care of it." The tears of emptiness overwhelmed me. To this day, I do not recall how I paid for my son's care. Times remained rough for a while. I had limited income, so the children got odd jobs to help with expenses. My father lived only 20 minutes away, but his second wife kept him away from me. Why was his character so weak that he couldn't bring himself to give me a $20 bill to help me feed my children? He didn't want to create waves with his wife, who was very domineering and didn't want to have anything to do with his children.

At one point, I found myself three months behind in rent and I knew I had nowhere to go. I was within a few days of being evicted when the phone rang.

"Hello, Devy, this is your Uncle Jim!" Uncle Jim was the ex brother-in-law of my father, divorced from Daddy's sister, my Aunt Edith. "Why are you crying, Devy? What's wrong?" I explained my situation and he asked for directions. Uncle Jim arrived that afternoon with a check for my delinquent rent and we stayed in close contact. It was good to renew the bond we had when I was young.

Uncle Jim had lived in Toledo Ohio and I'd take the B&O Railroad from Wilmington, Delaware to Defiance, Ohio to spend part of my summers with them. My cousins took me to 'teenage' parties and taught me to play golf. I was pretty good at it!

Many years later, Uncle Jim's health deteriorated and he needed care. His two sons showed no interest in helping him, so my husband, Phil, and I took him in. We put his house up for sale, paid his bills and took care of his affairs. I was at his side the night he died. I held his hand as he said he felt he was being pulled upward. He smiled, and told me of the brightness and beauty he was seeing. He was at peace. Uncle Jim had been there for me, when my own father refused to be. I was glad I was there for him, as he made his final transition.

What Comes Next?

"Drama is life with the dull bits cut out."
Alfred Hitchcock (1899-1980)

For those who think that divorce doesn't affect the children for long, I could write a script on the subject. Youngsters from a broken, fractured home *never* get over the ramifications of divorce. My children experienced abortion, sexual promiscuity, drugs and troubles with the law. Oh, how I wish my Lena Mae and my sister had been a part of my life when I needed family so desperately. In spite of the children's antics, I know that they would have been there for me. In fact, just knowing I had a sister would have given me great comfort. I needed to know I was not alone.

When my sweet Robin turned 18, she moved into her own apartment and got a job at a local hotel. The second child, Brooke, began his series of cross-country trips, running from here to there. His plan was that if he caused enough worry, his dad would eventually come home to us. It didn't work. Then there were the twins. Dirk, at 17 went into the Air Force. While at Travis Air Force Base in California, he was thrown by a horse and broke his back. Three months later he was healed and resumed his military service.

Darryl, his sister, worked at a local drug store to earn money for college. She entered Rollins College, in Central Florida, on a scholarship. She received more advantages than the other children, as her grandmother took her under her wing, gave her a car to drive and bought her college clothes. It was all in timing, I suppose. Robin had such artistic talent and was definitely college material, but her father refused to help her or any of the children. It hurt me deeply that I couldn't have been of more help to my children at this time, but my mind was focused on survival.

My next challenging job was to revamp the medical records department of a large clinic run by eight doctors. There were 57,000 patients on the rolls and 52 employees. It was within walking distance of home, a big plus. Many a Sunday, I would work all day, without pay, to accomplish a Herculean task, to sort out the veritable mess, which I found in most of the files. I spent 8 years there, and was proud of the job I did. The doctors all knew where things were and I could find anything a doctor needed and have it on his desk in seconds. The doctors gave me a hefty bonus when I left - I was getting married to one of our patients!

Our Time at the Beach

*"Either you decide to stay in the shallow end of the pool
or you go out in the ocean."*
Christopher Reeve

The apartment where my children and I lived was on the 10th floor of an 18 story building on the beach. My dear mother-in-law was on the 3rd floor. She faced the ocean - I faced the parking lot. Four nights a week, when I got home from the doctor's office, I'd fix her a tray of dinner and take it down to her. We'd have a drink together and then I'd go back to fix the children's supper. She and I were pals and our relationship remained exceptional until her death at 93.

Living on the ocean was great fun and it gave the children invaluable activities to share with others - water games in the huge pool and volleyball on the beach. I was amazed at the number of young people living there. However, this was in the 70s - life was a bit simpler.

There was a very nice dining room in the building along, with a bar and lounge and a bandstand for nightly music. I usually sat in the grillroom; the bartenders knew me and protected me from the 'wolves'. The owner gave me all the good leftovers from the kitchen and I made stews and soup for my children.

The New York Yankees held their spring training in Ft. Lauderdale and some of the players had apartments in our building. Whitey Ford, the pitcher, was very kind and we'd sit at the bar many a night and chat. If the band needed a little jolt, they'd ask me to sing with them. They knew of my singing at the old Bridge Restaurant.

Bill McPeak, a retired coach of the Washington Redskins also lived at the Royal Admiral. He was extremely respectful of me and very kind to my children.

Life Unexpected– Again!

"If one advances confidently in the direction of his dreams, and
endevours to live the life which he has imagined,
he will meet with a success unexpected in common hours."
Henry David Thoreau (1817-1862)

When one is quite content with life, when everything is going according to plan, something eventually comes along to upset the applecart. One of our patients from the doctor's office appeared one night in the Grille Room when I was having dinner. Our eyes met briefly and that was the end of it. I had seen him having dinner quite often, but he was always with a date. Then, early one morning as I was walking my little dog, this gentleman came jogging by. He stopped to say hello and introduced himself. His name was Phil. Before long, I would see him jogging every morning, same time, same place! We started dating and the rest, as they say, is history.

Years later, Phil related to me that when our eyes met in the Grille Room that first night, he wanted to know exactly who I was and if I lived in the building. He said my friends fiercely protected my privacy. Finally, after much persuasion, Leonard, our doorman told him that every morning before work I walked my dog in front of the building. So clever Phil decided to change his jogging route and come 5 miles up the beach to see me!

For a time, my life would be a bit complicated. I missed not having a mother to talk to at times like this. Mother had died and I wondered if my birth mama was still alive. I was sure she was, as I was only 43 at this point. I possessed some psychic abilities and often predicted future events with some success. Did Lena Mae Howell have the same psychic abilities? Could she know that I was alive and that we were connected on some level?

I was surely falling in love with Phil, a true Renaissance man. We were married on the beach at Lago Mar Resort one year later and began twenty-seven of the happiest years of my life. Phil had four grown children, as did I. Now we were a couple with four boys and four girls. Being a part of a large family was heaven to me. I instantly became a grandmother of nine and as the years passed, the family grew as the children married. Before long, there were 11 grandchildren and 10 great grandies.

I knew somewhere in my background I was predisposed to care for family and the joys a good family brings to each other. The need to care and nurture all living things has always been a part of my existence. Where did it come from, I've wondered?

Phil and Me on Our Honeymoon, 1982

It seemed idyllic to finally have a large family. I loved planning family parties, especially at Thanksgiving and Christmas. There were a few times when all the children and grandies came together and we had boat rides, Bar-B-Qs, marathon runs, swimming with the dogs in the pool and fishing off our dock. These were such happy family times and I reveled in the joy of family.

Phil catered to the large yachts and their crews during his twenty-eight years as owner of Bahia Mar Marine, Inc., a world-class yacht chandlery in a large marina in Ft. Lauderdale. He had wonderful employees and after we married I helped wherever needed, especially during the boat shows. It was fun place to be and our Labrador retriever, Samantha, was our mascot who greeted everyone, looking out after young children of the customers.

Phil left much of the daily running of the business to the employees as he pursued his favorite hobby and interest; that of aerobatic flying in competition.

The first time he took me up in his Pitts S-2B (biplane), we flew down to Key Biscayne, buzzing Richard Nixon's home. I could nearly reach through the canopy and touch the clouds. I truly thought I was in heaven and the butterflies in my stomach told me I was.

If only I had known that I had a sister and family in Tennessee, we could have shared all these fun experiences. But, destiny had other plans for Patricia Wilks and Devy Bruch.

Phil and Me, His "First Mate"

To France a la Bicyclette!

"Two roads diverge in a wood and I -
I took the one less traveled by . . ."
Robert Frost (1874-1963)

Shortly after my marriage to this dear spur-of-the-moment fellow, we bought two touring bikes, each with 18 speeds and very thin tires. Wouldn't it be fun to take our own bikes to France and ride through the wine country, through the Pyrenees Mountains and to the Spanish border, then back up the coast of France into Paris?

We chartered our course as we went, not on an organized tour, but by ourselves. We had trained for months, building up our leg muscles. One day we'd jog six miles (Phil would go farther); the next day we'd ride our bikes twenty-five miles. We were in good shape to tackle the hills of France. It was a phenomenal experience.

We stayed only at local places, tiny hostels where two people could relax for hours over a seven course dinner for about $8.00 American. The rooms were clean; the bathroom was at the end of the hall. My French got better with each day and the menus were easier to decipher.

We loved the French countryside. It was easy to get down little dirt roads where cars couldn't go. We explored so many areas and at the end of one of those little dirt roads was a gorgeous castle where Lord Byron had been chained to a pillar in a dungeon for 4 years. The old cracked furniture had cobwebs everywhere and the lovely grandfather clock must have chimed during another place in time, echoing throughout.

We were equipped for all eventualities, even a dental kit and sleeping bag, but we never used either. We carried two of Phil's silver cups, monogrammed of course, for our daily wine consumption. It was our only touch of class and the wine seemed to taste better. We had great fun eating and drinking our way along, never gaining an ounce. We usually rode 35 – 50 miles (not kilometers) daily.

Looking back we both felt that our five weeks biking through France was a holiday that we couldn't top.

Building a Home for Family and Friends

"Mid pleasures and palaces though we may roam,
be it ever so humble, there's no place like home."
John Howard Payne (1791-1852)

One of Phil's dreams remained. He confessed that he had accomplished all of his life's goals, except one - to build an authentic Georgian Colonial home with Pennsylvania Farmhouse features. We'd take the motorcycle or our bikes and buzz all over Fort Lauderdale, looking for the right spot, a place where we could build our home and harbor our boat safely from hurricanes. We found just the spot in a lovely old neighborhood on Tarpon River. There was a small bungalow on the property, built in 1939, which had to come down. It was on a double lot, which gave us enough space to build exactly the home Phil dreamed of.

We began this project in 1985, beginning with the 134 feet of dock with three power stations for visiting boats. That enabled us to bring our boat over to the site, live aboard, and watch our lovely home come to fruition. We moved in mid May of 1986 and for the next twenty years, we enjoyed a lifestyle, which we could have only dreamed of. The huge brick courtyard in the front could park fifteen cars. It served as the location for four beautiful weddings for our children and large parties with upwards of 430 people.

When the Whitbred Round the World Sailing race chose Ft. Lauderdale as its first U. S. port of call, we offered our home to entertain the crews from the nine participating nations. That was the largest party we ever had. The City officials loved it, as did all the sailors participating. We had a bar for each nation with their national flags flying. Costumed servers mingled about and a photographer hung out the 2nd floor windows to record the frivolity. This was 1990.

There were times when we enjoyed taking the boat out nearby and anchoring off the Intracoastal Waterway. No one knew where we were – no phone, no TV, just peace and quiet to watch the sun go down over the sea, as we enjoyed our cocktails on the back deck. We always enjoyed a nice supper, which I cooked aboard. The fireplace in the main salon had a dandy grill for cooking our meat. These were poignant times; we were so happy, crazy in love and we relished each day. Time became dearer when Phil developed serious health concerns.

I now know that during this time my birth mother, Lena Mae (then Pruett), was in a boarding home with fifteen other residents, in poor health and experiencing some confusion. She was having dinner on May 14th 1991 when she left the table to return to her room to write a letter. She didn't make it. Lena Mae collapsed and died of cardiac arrest on another resident's bed. If only I had authorized my daughter to begin her research of my beginnings sooner, perhaps my birth mother would have lived to hug the daughter that destiny took from her. I needed her hug.

Open Doors, Open Heart

"Let no one ever come to you without leaving better and happier."
Mother Teresa (1910-1997)

The entry gates to the courtyard and the service driveway kept the secrets and mysteries of friends and family well guarded. So many friends and acquaintances came to us in need. Some whom we harbored and protected, some we counseled and supported. Some stayed a few nights, others for a few years. But, all of their stories remain there and never went outside the gates. I suppose our place could have been called a five-star nursing home, but those who came never left hungry and were well rested and cared for before they left. Phil and I were a team – we helped each other with daily chores and responsibilities. We both felt that caring for others in need was an honorable act and in each case we rather enjoyed being able to help. Phil lived by the Golden Rule, I by my Quaker background. We complimented each other in all phases of our life together.

Phil and I Enjoyed Entertaining
Friends and Family in Our Home

To Marquette, Michigan, with Daddy

"So live that your memories will be part of your happiness."
Author Unknown

I took a trip to the town where Daddy grew up to bury my stepmother in the family plot. He took me all over, to the mines where his father worked as a mining engineer. As a child, I was enchanted by the stories of his travels to Cuba and the southwest to build railroads. Now, I was in the exact place where his career began, seeing the family homestead for the first time - a large red stone Victorian house with a cupola on the top. The stone to build it had come from the mine in Marquette. It was so large, with a huge, staircase winding up to three floors, that in later years it was divided into twelve apartments with two more apartments in the basement.

I was mesmerized at the thought of how Daddy grew up. I've seen the photos of the lawn parties the Rose family had, with women playing badminton on the lawn in their huge, bustled skirts and finery. Then there was Annie, the family cook, who served them well all through Daddy's life in Marquette. Aunt Edith Rose and Grandmother Florence Rose had all their dresses made by seamstresses who came for three weeks at a time, taking up residence until their jobs were compete. During those times, Daddy's sister and mother took the train to Chicago for a week or so to shop at Marshall Fields and Co. to restock the house in Marquette.

Godparents Come To Stay – For A Long While!

"Sure I'm helping the elderly.
I'm going to be old myself some day."
Lillian Carter, *in her 80s*

Aunt Grace and Uncle Meigs were my Godparents, whom I had known all my life. When I was a child, our family went to Washington, D. C. each year to visit them on Embassy Row in Bethesda. Uncle Meigs was a big deal in the State Department, a patent attorney and a naval officer, who spent much of his time traveling the world. Aunt Grace was a beautiful woman, a prima Dona who spent much of her days in bed reading and ordering fine things over the telephone. They had no children and were always interested in my life. My mother and Uncle Meigs had gone to George Washington University together. My parents were married in the Brearley home. It was a deep friendship of long standing.

Many years later, the Brearleys retired and built a home in Boca Raton, Florida, close to where I lived in Fort Lauderdale. I was aware that they were having health difficulties. Aunt Grace had developed a fear of anyone coming into their home to clean or assist them in any way.

One morning, as I was preparing to leave the house for the Marina Store with our yellow Labrador, Samantha, I received an eerie phone call. "Devereaux, your Uncle Meigs is on the floor and I can't get him up. I think he has been there for three days."

97

I went immediately to their aid. As I arrived at the guardhouse of their community, I told the guard to send an ambulance right away. What I found was definitely a medical emergency. Meigs was near death, in kidney failure, with other complications. Their 21 year-old Abyssinian cat was very hungry. Gracie was completely confused and unable to take charge. I wondered, "How do I split myself down the middle for this one?"

Uncle Meigs was stabilized on the spot and admitted to a local hospital where he remained for thirty days. I brought Aunt Grace and the cat home with me and got her settled in a bedroom. Each day, I fed and took care of her, then went back to the hospital to check on Meigs. Praise the Lord I had good help. Gisela, who was with us for many years, was my right hand and through the years I've loved her as my own family.

The doctors gave us a poor prognosis for each of them. Aunt Grace had had many strokes and was very soon bedridden. Uncle Meigs needed dialysis treatments three times a week, three hours a treatment. The cost was over $500 per treatment and the doctors loved seeing him come. He had the same insurance, as did members of Congress, 100% of all medical expenses were paid. Of course, Phil and I had no idea how long either would live. The doctors told us perhaps a year. Maybe a bit more. Phil was very supportive. We couldn't let them go home, where they had no one. I loved them and had such happy memories of their love for me. Of course it wasn't easy; they required round the clock care.

HELP!

"Only if we understand can we care.
Only if we care will we help."
Jane Goodall

Marva was a blessing from the Gods. She came to us through the Alzheimer's Association. Her recent charge had died and she was looking for work. Marva was well trained for the job she was about to undertake. She was clean, neat, capable, pleasant, dependable and a joy to have around. Marva was a good cook and an excellent caregiver. She kept Gracie very shined up. Grace never suffered from bedsores or rash because Marva kept her turned and active. She dressed her 'to the nines', put on her lovely picture hat and wheeled her out the door, through the courtyard and down the lovely, tree lined streets of our neighborhood. Everyone soon knew my Aunt Grace and she seemed very happy.

At the back of the house was a large dock, where Meigs and Grace would often sit together and watch the boats go by and the fish jump in the river. Their days were happy. They had their cocktails, chocolates, coffee laced with Drambuie, and so on; anything they wished. I took Uncle Meigs to the store with me so he could pick out things he liked. The months passed into years and the two of them fooled the doctors. They had received such good care that she lived three more years and he lived five years. We gave them a happy period toward the end of their lives.

What Alzheimer's Disease Took From Us

"As to disease make a habit of two things –
to help – to do no harm."
Hippocrates *(460 BC-337 BC)*

Alzheimer's is a horrific disease unlike any other. Many lay people say it's just a form of dementia, but it goes far beyond that. I began to notice changes in Phil's behavior, such as him putting our camera in the freezer, or a bar of soap in the toilet that created bubbling activity! Such things were out of character for him, yet he maintained his sweet, gentle personality.

Phil had also undergone several cancer surgeries, which were intertwined with his sometimes squirrelly behavior. His spirit remained ace high, and we were able to maintain some semblance of normal life: dinners out, small parties at home and taking the boat around the waterways in Fort Lauderdale. We often visited friends by boat, a way of life for most who live in the 'Venice of America'.

I learned the importance of playing along with Phil and to never get angry or cross. His behavior was the effect of an illness and he surely couldn't help it. Keeping a cheery, calm environment and giving him comfort whenever he needed it brought me great pleasure. True love is placing someone else's welfare above your own; I knew that keeping Phil at home, with his dogs and comforts, was essential to his well-being and the quality of his life.

One memorable day, Phil took his jeep to run an errand; it was one of the few times that he didn't take his dog along with him. Much time had passed, which caused me great concern. I was prepared to call the police because he had no cell phone with him and even if he had, I wasn't sure he'd be able to use it. Three and a half hours later, he came into the driveway. I was so happy to see him, but grew even more worried. He hadn't a clue where he had been, and couldn't tell me anything. At this point, I called the Mayo Clinic and we drove to Jacksonville the following week for a complete evaluation.

Our five days at the clinic gave me the diagnosis I needed to know. The tests were grueling for him - verbal, written, psychological and medical.

"Phil and Devy, it is no fun to tell a family that they will be living with Alzheimer's disease. You will have many decisions to make, "the doctor stated. "The first one must be that you, Phil, turn over the car keys to Devy. It is not safe for you to drive anymore." This is the only time I saw him get angry.

"But you don't know what a good driver I am" he exclaimed, "That's out of the question." .

I started volunteering with The Alzheimer's Association of South Florida, and the knowledge I gained was invaluable while caring for Phil as the disease progressed.

It took many months of role playing and praying that he wouldn't kill himself or someone else. In the meantime, he puttered about compulsively, cleaning the attic, the garage, his closets, over and over and over again. He kept putting items out by the fence for trash collection and anyone could pick up the nice things he was getting rid of. My bicycle disappeared, as did my good luggage, my jewelry, and items from our bathroom drawers. I couldn't follow him around every minute and many of our belongings he just threw away. The next important decision in our lives had to be made, and made soon.

Although Phil appeared lucid and cognizant most of the time, periods of squirrelly behavior continued. He could no longer take care of our home the way he had always done and it frustrated him.

During this time, my daughter Darryl called to tell us about a nice home that had been recently placed on the market in her neighborhood, about twenty-five minute drive north of us. On a lark, we drove up to see it. This new home would require some downsizing, but seemed an appropriate move for that point in our lives. We bought it the same day we saw it, and put the big house in Fort Lauderdale on the market.

It was a sad transition. We had put our souls into that house and felt we would live there forever. It's difficult to realize that things can't stay the same forever, but life must go on.

Our daughter Darryl and her family had led us to believe that they wanted us living closer to them so they could look in on us. It was a good arrangement and we enjoyed being nearby and sharing family events. But this arrangement was very short lived. Darryl and her husband decided to move to Georgia to be near their good friends. It was a good move for them, but we were very much alone in a new house in a new neighborhood. We weren't happy after they left and Phil deteriorated quickly.

Saying Goodbye to Our Home

"The wisdom of life consists
in the elimination of nonessentials."
Lin Yutang

We had a farewell party, just to let our friends know that we would only be forty minutes away by car. It was a bittersweet event, nostalgic in many ways. Phil had been diagnosed with Alzheimer's disease, not leprosy, but many of our friends left us by the wayside and soon forgot us after we left the area. Fair weather friends, and now the weather was stormier. It was a difficult time. I had been abandoned so many times before: taken from my natural mother at birth, given the cold shoulder for 20 years by my adopted father, left stranded by my first husband and now by the friends whom I thought were as close to me as family. Who could I count on? Was there a real family somewhere who would care for me and not abandon me again? I've run the gamut of emotions over this for many years.

Life in Peachtree City, Georgia

"Waste not fresh tears over old griefs."
Euripides, (484 BC-406BC)

We arrived at our Georgia home on Pearl Harbor Day - December 7th, 2006. We walked in the front door to discover that my daughter Darryl had placed most of the furniture and set up a beautiful Christmas tree, which was decorated with tiny white lights that shone brightly. Phil was so happy. We felt at home when the neighbors came to welcome us. What a special way to begin the Christmas season, our first in Georgia.

Phil seemed to thrive. There was so much for him to see, as we'd walk the dogs through the woods down to the lake each day. Tara, our Labrador, loved swimming in the lake. We were in the process of putting in a pool and waterfall out back. This was a wonderful chance for Phil to supervise the construction; he relished every aspect of the building and enjoyed having his lunch outside so he could continue watching every moment of the process.

Once the pool was completed, it was heartrending to see Phil in the pool with his dog. Phil had always been a very good swimmer but with Alzheimer's disease and his lack of memory, he could forget the simplest functions and remembering how to swim could be one of them. I held a watchful eye over him.

Peaceful Peachtree City, Georgia – Our New Home

As the weeks passed, Phil and I settled into a comfortable routine, being with the children and exploring our new community. Our routine was simple; Phil enjoyed his comforts and the foods he liked and could tolerate.

Cocktail time was always an important part of our day from our dating days. We'd drop everything to sit together and go over the events of the day, what we had done, and our plans, laughing over silly things while we nursed our drinks and little snacks.

By this time, Phil had become very repetitive. I listened patiently to the same things over and over and over again, pretending that I was hearing each story for the first time. This was the key to my survival.

Alzheimer's disease is a hideous, horrific condition. Everyone's degree of illness is different. I'd heard the stories of some who faced great abuse from belligerent spouses, making it impossible to care for them at home.

Although my situation was hard at times, Phil never became abusive. It was always my mindset to keep him in his own cozy environment, knowing that he would live a more productive and happy life with his comforts and dogs. Home is where the heart is and our hearts remained intertwined until he ascended, in peace, to his final resting place - only six months after we arrived in Georgia.

More of Robin's Story, A Mystery Solved

"A man travels the world over in search of what he needs
and returns home to find it."
George Moore

As a flight attendant, whenever I had a Memphis layover I would think about my real relatives. Were they close by, did they still live in the area? I wanted to know. I would look at people on my flights in and out of Memphis to see if anyone looked familiar - like me! But, I could not do anything more because my mother said 'no'. After all these years, she still did not want to hurt her father's feelings.

Here I am With My 'Detective' Daughter,
Robin Bunch

When the movie 'Stolen Babies' came out, starring Mary Tyler Moore as Georgia Tann, my curiosity was piqued. This was in 1994. My Mom could have been one of the children stolen by the evil Georgia Tann. This was the first time I had heard of Georgia Tann and the stolen babies in Memphis. Nevertheless, the answer from Mom was still 'no, do not open a complex issue'. I don't know why Mom felt that way. However, I respected her decision.

My mother's adoptive father was still alive. As said before, she did not want to hurt him…Lordy—I do not know why! He had hurt her plenty in the last several years. I really think she was intimidated by him her whole life, as I was. Therefore, we waited, and time went on.

I found an article in the Ladies Home Journal on Georgia Tann in 1996. I cut it out and gave it to my mother. Finally, her interest was piqued. She took the article to her father and he confirmed it after all these years: "Yes, we adopted you from Georgia Tann." Wow, we finally had an answer, a place to start. Nevertheless, ten more years would pass before I got an okay to begin looking.

Time is both a revealer and a robber of important things in life. If we had started in the 1980s, looking for our family, my mother would have met her real Mom, Lena Mae. You never know, but it could have given Lena Mae a will to live longer than she did. Just speculation, something to think about. Don't waste precious time.

In April 2009, I bought the book "The Baby Thief" by Barbara Bisantz Raymond, the same woman who wrote the Ladies Home Journal article more than ten years prior. It was such a well-written and precise book that I devoured it. I then sent it to my Mother asking finally if I could have her records opened. The answer was finally, "Yes, see what you can find…."

I had my Mom FAX all the adoption information she had. When her father passed away she found all this information in a dusty file hidden deep in the bowels of his musty apartment.

On Sunday, April 19, 2009, I did a Google search. First I typed in "Georgia Tann Adoptions." Then, "Adoption Records, Tennessee." Quickly I got a name with the e-mail address @state.tn.us. So blindly I sent an e-mail. This is my letter sent at 7:59 PM PST on April 19th.

> *Dear Mr._____ ,*
> *This is an inquiry on how to find an illegal adoption record for my mother born in Shelby County, Memphis in late 1937. Her adoptive father just passed away and gave her a paper stating her adoption was by a Miss Georgia Tann. We would like to find some record of her family for medical and other reasons.*
>
> *We know of this awful record of stealing children and it is sad, to say the least. The story is that she arrived by a big black limo on Christmas Day, with Miss Georgia*

Tann delivering her personally. If it might help at all, her birth record says born 11/02/1937.

  Can you please tell us where to even start finding a record?

Thank you for any info and time.
Robin Bunch

I added my address and phone number. Promptly the next morning, I got a return e-mail. The woman said that she forwarded my e-mail to the folks in 'Post Adoptions" to address my questions and that I should be hearing from them shortly. She also gave me a website with the forms I needed to fill out to get the ball rolling. One hour later I got an e-mail from a woman in 'Post Adoptions' at the Department of Children's Services in Nashville, Tennessee. She said to phone her for instructions on requesting access to your mother's adoption record. I called right away. I needed to write a letter with

  1- My Mother's name
  2- Birthdate
  3- Adoptive parents complete names
  4- City and County in TN where she was born

She gave me the correct address at the Department of Children's Services in Nashville. I had that address memorized by the time this was finished. We had a lot of back and forth correspondence over the next two months.

I believe that after I sent the information in my first letter, the department searched to see if there was actually a record of my mother's birth. I then received a letter stating that there was a fee of $150 to determine my eligibility for this service. I also had to send them my birth certificate, marriage license, a photo I.D. They needed proof of my relationship to my mother. Now the process was beginning. It was very exciting - I could hardly wait each week to hear from Tennessee! A lot of information went back and forth. After a month, I called them and asked, "Have you found anything at all?"

"Oh, yes, we have found 82 pages of records and photographs." What?! I was wondering what could 82 pages hold? But first, they would need a fee of $20.50. Twenty-five cents per page for copying. ($15.00 for the sealed adoption agency record and $5.50 for the post adoption file). I thought, 'well... we've waited this long, what is another week?'

What a long week it was... June 22, 2009, two months and 2 days after I began this quest, the certified envelope came.

Coming Full Circle

"Love is like a tree, it grows of its own accord,
it puts down deep roots into our whole being."
Victor Hugo *(1802-1885), Notre-Dame de Paris*

Very little is known of my birth father, except his name: Gaston Gann, age, 23. What was he like? Was his character strong and precocious like mine? I'm suspecting that Mama, Lena Mae, was a kind loving soul. She had to be; I see those traits in my sister, Pat. So many things in my life, the experiences, the places I've been, the people whose lives have touched mine, have made me wonder and intrigued me. Who am I? How was my character molded?

My Mama, Lena Mae Howell, in the 1930s

117

My wonderful family who chose me to be their daughter worked hard to teach me important lessons. They told me that life can be tough, but we must deal head on with problems and do our level best to solve them. I always tried to face things head on and not push them under the rug, as if they didn't exist. Learning good sense in handling money was part of their teaching.

They came out of the depression and the great generation of the World War II. Life was simpler then. Families loved each other and cared for the infirm. There were no nursing homes to scuttle the older folks in the family off to. Grandma lived with us and we loved and cared for her until her death. Her wisdom provided some interesting conversations, and I felt as though she added a meaningful dimension to my life. Her name was Emma Agnes O'Brien Kelly. She was a good Catholic and bore five children; my mother was her last child.

When I had my twins, I wondered if there was any history of multiple births from my birth family. Then, it hit me: Could I be a twin? Could there be two of us? Now that I knew I had a sister, I had to know her age, her date of birth, as soon as possible!

My Mama in the Late 1930s

Family at Last

*"The happiest moments of my life have been the few which I
have passed at home in the bosom of my family"*
Thomas Jefferson *(1743-1826)*

At 71 years of age, I learned that I had a sister and a real, caring, loving family. Nothing in my life has affected me so deeply. It turned my life around. I now realize that I spent many years craving a big family. I always opened up my home to everyone, and provided a warm, cozy place for people to enjoy good food and drink. This was my way of creating family. I reached out to my confidants, my friends, and invited them into my heart, but all in their own way, drifted apart from me. The feat of abandonment was present in my life, but no more.

The Howells of Tennessee are my people, my blood, my family. The love they have given me and the knowledge that we are one has brought me a joy and fulfillment I never imagined was possible. There is no denying my roots; the resemblance to them is unmistakable.

The Howell Family History
as Told to Me by My Sister, Patricia Wilks

"There are two lasting bequests we can give our children.
One is roots. The other is wings."
Hodding Carter Jr.

The Howells came to America from Wales in the 17th century. They were known as horse thieves and run out of the country. Mother's lines date back to 1796. Her ancestors, Sarah and Abraham Howell, walked to Tennessee from South Carolina in 1796. Sarah stayed with friends in Linden, TN while Abraham went to Monroe County, MS to stake a land claim, then returned for Sarah. They were the first white settlers in the county. They had 18 children. Abraham staked his claim to several hundred acres of land in the center of Monroe County, MS.

The peaceful possession of the new land did not last long. Abraham might be considered a squatter, taking possession of land, as there were no others to claim it. The government began issuing surveys and patents, and folks came to claim the land that was staked out by Abraham Howell. The land was surrendered, but giving it up for the future did not occur to him. As opportunity presented itself, Grandfather Howell bought back the acres Abraham had lost. The first Warranty Deed to 80 acres is recorded in the year 1826.

My Grandparents' Home, Where They Raised Six Children

Several hundred more acres were added in the years that followed. The land is still in the possession of the descendants of Abraham Howell, who lost his original stake but wouldn't give up.

Abraham died in 1867 at age 75, the year following the Civil War. Sarah lived to be 84, passing away in 1878. She was well remembered by her grandchildren for the stone pipe she smoked, a common practice for older women at that time. She could not read, but enjoyed her children reading the Bible to her. The Howells were traditional Methodists.

Our patriarch, James Gilbert Howell, M. D. ("never make love in a buggy, for horses carry tales") was a direct descendant of Sarah and Abraham Howell and was known as "the horse doctor." He practiced in Enville, TN, a tiny town of about 200 people. Enville is at best a wide place in the road. There were four churches then. The town now consists of a bank, a post office and one store. There are a few other buildings that are in a state of collapse. Patricia relates that when she was young and living in Enville, these old buildings were stores. "The town was the most boring place in the world, but we didn't know any better; it was where we lived."

Lena Mae on Her Mother's Lap

The eminent doctor, known to the family as Papa Howell, practiced medicine in a rural area where great poverty existed. Everyone was in the same boat; no one knew they were poor. Dr. J. G would strap his medicine bags to his saddle and ride wherever his medical services were needed. The barter system was alive and well in Tennessee in those days and Papa Howell was paid in produce, eggs or a chicken - whatever the patient had on hand. Women who had "female problems" were hesitant to tell the good doctor what was really wrong, yet he seemed to know and treated them with a teaspoon of sugar and a shot of whiskey -his remedy for menopause.

On many occasions Papa Howell would hook his horse to a wagon and travel over the town bridge while escorting his choice of lady at the time. The horse was trained to stop at a certain point on the bridge, to allow J. G. time for smooching and a touch of intimacy.

Doc Howell had an eye for one Miss Maggie Jones. Maggie's father was Henry Booker Bascomb Jones who had a houseful of beautiful daughters. He was so strict and stern that almost everyone was afraid of him. Papa Howell went on to marry Hannah Gibson and they had two little boys, Carl and Earl. Hannah died of a fever when the boys were small. Doc married a second time, but while delivering a son, complications resulted in the death of both mother and child. Carl and Earl disliked the second wife and recalled that she dressed them in white suits and spanked them when they got dirty.

Grandmother Maggie Howell

Doc Howell was my grandfather. His untimely death on May 7th, 1936 preceded my birth by eighteen months. He contracted pneumonia and passed away at 58 years of age. His severe arthritis and heart problems have given me a window into my own health history for the first time. I've never known a thing about my health background.

James Gilbert Howell eventually went back to his first sweetheart, Maggie Jones, who was 35 years old and an old maid. She gave him six children in quick succession, the last born when she was 46. One died as an infant and the last born, Martha, was autistic. Mama Howell was a kind, loving, motherly type who, I've been told, would have loved and welcomed me.

Maggie Howell holding my mother, Lena Mae

Little Nell Howell was her first grandchild, but she never knew it. One can imagine how she suffered when Papa Howell died at 58, leaving her relatively destitute.

It was in this difficult environment that Lena Mae, my mother, would seek some joy and love and perhaps an easier life with a 23 year-old employee in the circulation department of the local newspaper. Mr. Gaston Gann was my father. Very little is known about him or if he ever knew Lena Mae carried his child.

During the Great Depression, it was shameful to be pregnant and unwed. The records indicate that no one knew of Lena Mae's pregnancy, except her half-brother, Earl Howell, who drove her to

Memphis. He knew of a home for unwed girls there, run by a woman named Georgia Tann. Lena Mae told her family that she was going to Memphis to beauty school. Earl was sworn to secrecy and never told anyone about Lena Mae's situation.

She entered Georgia Tann's boarding house for unwed girls. I can only speculate as to how she was treated. Did she make friends? Was she comfortable? Was she well cared for? The records indicate that she paid no money for her entry or care. However, it became well known years later that Ms Tann's charged exorbitant fees to adoptive parents which covered all her costs, plus the kickbacks and bribes she paid to all city officials, enabling her to continue her criminal enterprise.

It appears that there was no discussion regarding the baby Lena Mae delivered. Why would there have been if she was told that her boy baby had died at birth. Pat, born six years later after Lena married, confessed that our mother had a very sad life.

Often, Pat saw her mother staring in deep thought, looking sad. When Pat questioned Mama, she just blew it off as nothing. Pat feels strongly that Mama often wondered about her baby that had died. It was a viable, live baby kicking inside of her; how could it have been born dead?

Grandma Howell in Her Garden

Patricia's World

". . . we shall pay any price, bear any burden, meet any
hardship, support any friend, oppose any foe,
to assure - survival and success . . . ".

John F. Kennedy (1916-1963)

Lena Mae Howell married John Biven Richardson on June 27th, 1942. Pat was born on September 24th, 1943. The wedding took place in Corinth, MS at the home of friends. Shortly thereafter, they went to Hartsville, TN, John's hometown, about fifty miles northeast of Nashville. The bridegroom was a very charming, handsome man, but an alcoholic. Lena Mae didn't truly understand the implications of this disease, or perhaps wasn't aware of it prior to the marriage. A wonderful person he was, when sober, yet he turned ugly when drinking.

Patricia Ann at 6 months of Age

Patricia Ann Richardson at 15 Months of Age

The marriage ended when Patricia was just 3½ years of age. Lena Mae mustered up a lot of courage to leave; she probably felt they were both in danger. He died at age 40 and mother and daughter were relieved they didn't have to be afraid of him anymore.

Lena Mae was Mama Howell's second child. After the separation from her husband, they went to Enville, TN to live with Mama Howell and Martha, the youngest child, born when Mama was 46. As the years went by, Pat was learning her chores well. From the time she was four years old, she walked to the little white house across the dirt road to get buckets of water to supply the needs of Mama Howell's house. They had no running water, no heat, no air-conditioning, somewhat primitive, yet almost everyone in Enville lived that same way. They were happy and never realized they were poor.

The garden they nurtured provided a bounty of food, which they canned all summer so that they had food for the winter. Patricia learned early how to split logs and carry them in to the wood stove for heat during the winter.
Pat walked to Enville grade school, "It was the kind of school you read about; all 8 grades in three rooms," she related.

When it came time for high school, Pat rode the bus to Henderson, TN, sixteen miles away. They had no car or transportation, so if she missed the bus, she was stuck. Looking back in retrospect, she smiles, remembering that their idea of security was putting the latch on the screen door.

Patricia graduated from high school in 1961. That was the same year that I had my twins. How sad that we missed so many important occasions in each of our lives, never having the opportunity to share laughter and love.

In the early 1960s, there wasn't much to do in Enville, TN, so Pat and a friend caught a ride to Memphis. They had a difficult decision, whether to go to Nashville or Memphis. Pat's friend had a cousin coming to Memphis and that's how they ended up there.

Pat's High School Graduation

With some monetary gifts at graduation, Pat enrolled in a business college and got a part-time job at Sears' mail order department. She needed her job and worked very hard at it.

Patricia and her friend Peggy were not accustomed to city life; they were country girls. Their first home was a studio apartment, with a bedroom, a bath and a kitchen. This was home and they were pleased with it.

"Being in the city was so new to us and we weren't used to the noise. Every time we heard a siren, we ran to see what was going on.

"My job at Sears went so well that they kept me on after the Christmas holidays. It lasted for 7 years, until 1968 when our son, Clinton, was born."

"During the spring of 1962 I met Eddie Wilks. He seemed a bit older and had just gotten out of the Navy. He was working at a car dealership and taking accounting courses part-time at the same business college I attended. Neither one of us knew our way around Memphis very well. On Valentine's Day 1963 we bought a set of rings and decided to make a life together. The rings were beautiful, but we were in debt for the first time and it worried us."

"Our wedding was on Saturday, August 24, 1963 at Madison Heights Methodist Church chapel. It was a small affair with just Mother and a few aunts and uncles. We left for a honeymoon in Gatlinburg."

My sister Pat Wilks with her husband, Eddie

"Two children have blessed our marriage, James Clinton, born July 8, 1968 and Lara Christine, born August 12, 1970. Christine has a daughter, Samantha Ann, born September 23, 1990. Now Samantha has a son, Connor Scott Keenum, born May 2nd, 2008. This now makes my younger and only sister a great grandmother at 66."

Pat and Eddie

Lena Mae's Passion

*"Beautiful young people are accidents of nature,
but beautiful old people are works of art"*
Eleanor Roosevelt

I believe that old-fashioned hand-done embroidery
is a dying art. I'm certain that I inherited my
mother's artistic skills, with my love for knitting.
Lena Mae made beautiful quilts, some patchwork,
some appliquéd or embroidered. My sister chose
not to do embroidery; there was so much of it
around her. She chose another skill, that of a crafter.
Her button-art sells well at the many annual craft
shows they attend. But, our mother's quilts were the
talk of the town; they were her claim to fame.

In 1959, Lena Mae decided to marry a second time.
Her family felt it was a bad move, but her motives
may have been compelled by a fear of growing old
alone. Patricia felt it was the case. Before long, her
new husband presented serious character flaws; she
was in a challenging situation. When neither he nor
Mama was doing very well health-wise, his family
put him in the hospital and Patricia went to get our
mother. Mama lived with Pat and Eddie for a
couple of years. However, it became increasingly
more difficult to care for her. She was overweight,
had a pacemaker and suffered periods of confusion.
Lena Mae went to live in a nice boarding house
environment where there were 15 other residents. It
appeared that she received good care.

On May 14th, 1991, Lena Mae left the dinner table
to write a letter. She never made it to her room,

having collapsed on another resident's bed, her heart stopping. Her burial place in Mt. Zion Cemetery in the little town of Enville, Tennessee is a most fitting resting place for her now to have eternal life. God bless you, Mama.

Sister, Pat, and Me at Mama's Gravesite

In Pat's Words, by Patricia Wilks

"In three words I can sum up everything I've learned about life:
It goes on."
Robert Frost (1874-1963)

I will remember the year 2009 always as a year of changes. The old saying one door closes and another opens comes to mind. In April, a door closed when my job was eliminated and I was escorted out of the building after many years.

On July 3, my cousin from Richmond, VA called to say she was working on our family history. I was surprised since I hadn't heard from her in a number of years. She had lots of questions about my family but mostly about my mother.

On July 9, my cousin called again and told my husband, Eddie, she'd found out I have a sister. She'd talked to other members of the family and they didn't know how to tell me. He told her I was a grown up person, turned away from the phone and repeated what she'd said. My answer "There is no way. You can forget this". Eddie asked my cousin if she had emails she could send us.

A new very, very emotional door had opened and I was in total shock. Within five minutes I was on the phone with my daughter, Christine, asking who she thought these people were and what did they want. I had so many questions. I told her emails were being sent. She told me I should wait until I felt like reading the emails - even if it was a few days - and go from there. It was kind of a "Mom, take one thing at a time" approach.

After three days I sent Devy an email thinking I should at least tell her a bit about myself. My first email started out "I have absolutely no idea what to say to you". It was true. I must have spent three hours writing and deleting. As soon as I sent the email, I noticed there was one from her.

We sent information back and forth, exchanged pictures and talked on the phone about the book she was writing. She and my new niece, Robin, came to Memphis on December 4. Eddie and I were to be at Homewood Suites at 4:30pm to meet them with Fox 13 News filming it.

I've never been an emotional person and have gone years without shedding a tear over anything. This year I've shed buckets of tears or so it seems. For our first meeting, I'd planned to be upbeat and friendly then ended up shedding more tears all over again. I saw Devy standing there and all I could think of was that it was meant to be. We resembled each other in lots of ways - this sister that Georgia Tann had deprived me of knowing.

My Sister and I Meet for the First Time,
December 4, 2009

The next day, December 5, we went to Mt. Zion cemetery near Enville, TN to visit mother's grave. This was also an emotional time. We decorated all of the Howell graves. The cemetery is very old and I tried to tell them some of the history. I somehow felt like mother knew we were there and approved.

LENA MAE HOWELL
PRUETT
JAN. 8, 1918
MAY 14, 1991

Mama's Grave Marker

I never knew mother was pregnant as a teenager. It was something the family never talked about. I even called a cousin I'd grown up with asking if he'd ever heard any talk. I'd always been an only child. One day I looked at my husband and said "Eddie, I have nieces and nephews". It was as if it had just hit me.

To me the saddest thing is that mother lived and died never knowing she had a little girl that was "out there" and thriving. Sometimes there was such sadness about her. I'd always ask what was wrong and she'd say nothing. I think I know now where the sadness came from.

This is an ongoing story. I look forward to meeting the rest of Devy's family. I think they will enjoy meeting my son, daughter, son-in-law, granddaughter and great-grandson.

Patricia Richardson Wilks
April 1, 2010

Adoption Not a Perfect Process

"Perfection is achieved, not when there is nothing more to add, but when there is nothing left to take away."
Antione de Saint-Exupery, French writer, (1900-1944)

I grew up in what many would consider an idyllic childhood. I knew I was special, I had been chosen. I had so many comforts - toys, dolls and trips to the hairdresser every few months for a permanent wave in my hair. My hair was straight as a poker. The style of the times was wavy hair, but mine was straight. I was just 5 or 6 when Mama began having hot rollers in my hair. I hated it and I rebelled once too strongly.

"Devereaux, stop it now or I might send you right back where we got you from." I know Mother regretted that remark, but that horrifying thought permeated my brain for a long time. Would I end up back in an orphanage?

Once, I rebelled when Mother made me wear brown oxford shoes with laces. All the other girls were wearing 'penny' loafers. "They are bad for your feet", Mother said. I hid the oxfords in the barn and refused to go to school. I sat there all day with my horse then, after school was dismissed, I walked up the driveway as though I had been at school. I remember thinking that my 'real' mother would have understood.

A Poignant Moment for Me at Mama's Gravesite

Actually, I thought about my 'real' mother often. On my birthday, I always wondered where she was and what she was doing, but I kept those thoughts to myself. Why upset the apple cart? I was very fortunate and I was happy. Yet, alone with my thoughts, I wondered what my mother looked like. How old was she when she gave me up for adoption? Was she still alive? Did she ever get to hug me? Did she get to say 'goodbye' to me?

Through it all, I never thought my life was unique or unusual. There were times when folks would ask me about how I felt about being adopted? Quite frankly, I thought it was a wonderful thing for a family to take a baby or child who had no home and provide one. Giving up a baby for a better life was a noble thing, I felt.

Who is Accountable to These Children
and Their Families?

"A person may cause evil to others not only by his actions
but by his inaction, and in either case,
he is justly accountable to them for the injury."
John Stuart Mill *(1806-1873)*

I was taping a promotional TV show about the Georgia Tann story and my family reunification for the Atlanta Market during February 2010. When I finished, one of the cameramen came up to me excitedly saying, "I was born in Memphis. I grew up there. Everyone knew of that horrible Georgia Tann lady. I never thought I'd ever meet someone whose life she touched."

Georgia Tann's Home Society

I recall reading in Barbara Raymond's book, The Baby Thief, how she tried to trace the steps and events of Georgia Tann's life and crimes. Barbara went to Memphis to talk to neighbors and folks who would have remembered Georgia Tann. The whole Memphis area seemed to protect her, perhaps afraid of reprisal, and no one wanted to talk. Barbara Raymond hit a brick wall over and over again. Greed and money and inflated egos contributed to the success of Georgia Tann's monumental criminal enterprise, which ran from 1925 – 1950. Bribes and kickbacks to those in high places were routine events of the time. No one was ever prosecuted for her horrific crimes of baby stealing, kidnapping, and trafficking in human life

Going through the eighty-two pages of my adoption records, I began to wonder what was done with all 'unadoptable' children, to the babies with birth defects, those that were not the right 'look'? What happened to the babies that Georgia Tann could not market, could not sell? I was one of the fortunate ones who fit her needs, blond, blue-eyed and female.

After Georgia Tann died in 1950, a common grave was discovered in the backyard of her home, a grave that held the remains of forty infants. When I realized that, I was shocked. How did these babies die? Did she smother them? Did her staff murder these infants? Each of these children was discarded with no name, no records, and no one who cared enough to protect and save them from Georgia Tann. I wonder if anyone even knew that those babies existed. Who were they? Who were their parents? Their families? I could have easily been one of those babies.

Each time a baby was torn from his or her natural mother, it was a deliberate and heinous act. These were intentional acts of cruelty and indifference. State and local systems and individuals denied these frail, tiny human beings their basic rights. Greed and corruption failed all of us who were touched and manipulated by Georgia Tann and the state of Tennessee. Why, we were nothing more than a commodity to Ms. Tann, just like a pair of shoes on the shelf, waiting to be selected and shipped away for the right price.

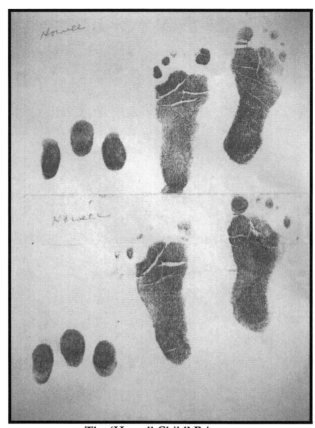

The 'Howell Child' Prints –
My Prints Discovered After 7 Decades!

Devy Through the Looking Glass

"The real man smiles in trouble, gathers strength from distress, and grows brave by reflection."
Thomas Paine (1737-1809)

If I were to step out of my life and see myself from the time I was a little girl until the present, what would I see? How have I been moved by my unusual life? Perhaps in more ways than I could ever imagine.

Patricia and I would have grown up as best friends. Together, we would help with the family chores, cut sticks of wood for the two stoves to heat our house in the wintertime and carry water from the neighbor's to help Mama Howell (our grandmother) and our mother, Lena Mae, with the washing and cleaning (Mama did not have running water). Through mother's gift and love of crafts and quilt making, I'm sure we would have learned to make our own dolls and they, in turn, would become our playmates.

Our personalities are different, Pat's and mine, but we complement each other. I, have a more devilish soul than my sister Pat, with her calm, easygoing demeanor. Together, we would have explored every inch of Enville, TN, taken in all stray animals and had a close knit, caring family to nurture us. We would have been content with what we had because we would have known nothing else; there would have not been any other point of reference. We would have never known we were poor.

But, how would we measure our wealth? Maybe by how many coins were in our piggy banks or how many dresses we shared that hung in our closet. Or, how hard we worked to nurture a garden to have enough to eat. I doubt we would have ever thought about it. The Howell family took care of its own throughout the generations. Family members were expected to help, whatever they were able to do, to assist the family as a unit.

For their entertainment and relaxation, they read books by the fire and talked to each other. Would I have been happy in the family? Would I have been free to develop my own personality? Yes, of course I would if only I had been given the chance. My origins are here, my mother, my family. The way my birth relatives have welcomed me into the fold is the most endearing experience of my life.

Now, let's look at another phase of my life, that of affluence and privilege and the opportunity to satisfy a quest for learning. How blessed I was in so many ways. My caring, educated parents, who chose me, helped me grow and develop the strong character I have today. Oh, at times I rebelled against their discipline, as I suppose most adolescents do. But, as I matured, I knew they were right and always had a reason and good explanation for what they did. I especially thank my mother for my speech and vocabulary. I remember that she would stop me in the middle of a sentence if my pronouns were incorrect.

"Stand up straight, Devereaux, no hunching over. Always sit with your legs together, as young ladies should." Her influence on my life was positive. She taught me a solid value system and character traits that helped me down the path of my life. I, in turn, have passed many of her lessons along to my children.

My Adoptive Parents, Janet and Bob Rose, in 1948

Daddy was as stern as he could be and was so disciplined; there was only one way to do things - the right way. His teachings have benefited me in most everything I do, especially the handling of money. Daddy lived a good, long, productive life to age 93. He passed peacefully in 1997 and was laid to rest in Birmingham-Lafayette Cemetery next to Mother, adjoining his beloved Linden Farm.

And now, another generation comes along, one sometimes foreign to my beliefs and upbringing, which can be difficult to understand. The "me – first" generation is still alive and well. Driven by greed and possessions, the shallow character of some folks who are now in my life saddens me greatly. It seems that they learned no values, focusing on what is in it for them. No spirituality, little substance. How can one be significantly fulfilled in any phase of life when roots are so shallow?

A study done by the Brookings Institute has shown that an increase in wealth produces no measurable increase in overall happiness. Statistics show that winning the lottery doesn't produce lasting gains in well-being. Most people vastly overestimate the extent to which more money would improve their lives. I've always looked at wealth as a tool for helping others, and that benefits me as well as them.

To my dear sister, who has been happily married for 47 years and has raised two great children, Christine and Clinton, may we live long enough to enjoy many years together now that we have finally found each other. Mama would like that.

As I write my story, flashbacks surface and tears come to my eyes. Throughout my life, I have tried to never look back – it's too painful. How did I endure it all, so alone in my daily struggle to survive? I held the light of God within and had Him sitting on my shoulder. I remembered how the Quakers, in their goodness, had helped me by feeding us and supporting us spiritually.

When I sat at Mama Lena Mae's gravesite in Enville, Tennessee, I felt an overwhelming sense that she knew I was there. That she knew I had lived. That her little baby had come home to see her.

"No Mama, I didn't die."

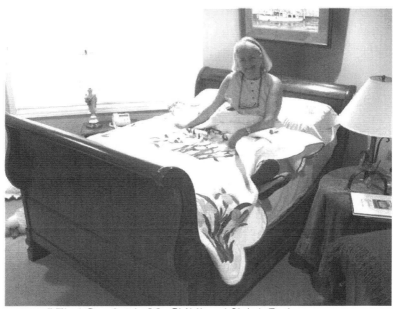

**I Find Comfort in My Childhood Sleigh Bed
with the Quilt Mama Sewed**

Epilogue

"Finish each day and be done with it. You have done what you could. Some blunders and absurdities no doubt crept in; forget them as soon as you can. Tomorrow is a new day; begin it well and serenely and with too high a spirit to be encumbered . . .".

Ralph Waldo Emerson

In one of the most heinous yet widely unknown periods of American history, from the mid-1920s through 1950, Georgia Tann kidnapped, stole and sold infants and children to wealthy families across the country. Most of the children came from poor, uneducated mothers who were told that Tann and her agency, the Tennessee Children's Home Society, would care for the children until these mothers could do so themselves. Mothers were told that their child appeared sickly and needed medical care. Tann then offered to provide medical attention and, if the parent refused, would threaten to have the parents declared unfit by the courts.

Under duress and fear, intimidated mothers signed away the rights to their children, thinking the document was to assign temporary care to Tann. When victimized mothers came back to claim their children, many were often told that the children had died from an illness. Others were shown the 'surrender documents' that had been signed earlier in confusion. It was later learned that dozens of children had died under Tann's charge and were unceremoniously buried in unmarked mass graves at the Home Society's Memphis location.

But, one must wonder how such an operation could exist in America. Georgia Tann had help in high places. Tennessee Judge Camille Kelly was the first female Juvenile Court judge in the south and the second in the US. With determination and drive, soon she became a judge for the Shelby County Family Court. It's unclear when Kelly and Tann became cohorts. In her role as child custody judge, Kelly could award guardianship of any child to Tann's Tennessee Children's Home Society. Perhaps, in the beginning, Kelly truly believed that a legal adoption would result. For her part, Tann received only a seven-dollar fee for each adoption arranged within the state of Tennessee. Quickly, she learned that adoptions out of state could generate much higher revenue. She often collected thousands per child. State records indicate that a percentage of these exorbitant fees were shared with Judge Kelly.

In the public eye, Tann and Kelly were viewed as advocates for unwanted children; Tann was often noted for her devotion to children. First lady Eleanor Roosevelt visited Judge Kelly and wrote of this visit in her "My Day" column on November 22, 1937.

"Sunday—There is nothing southern about Memphis . . . in order to do just a few of the things that were suggested to me, all of which I would have liked to do, I had to move quickly . . . I started for Judge Camille Kelly's Juvenile Court. There was no session today but I had always wanted to see where this only woman judge of a Juvenile Court in the south presided. It was a cheerful homelike building and one where I imagine a woman like Judge Kelly can do the kind of work that she thinks should be done to save the youth of this country from slipping down grade."

156

By the 1940s, Tann's practices faced scrutiny. Folks wondered how Tann could afford her large home and expensive chauffeur-driven cars while operating a charitable organization. Although the Child Welfare League of America withdrew its endorsement of the Tennessee Children's Home Society in 1941 due to lack of transparency within the agency, Tann defended her organization by declaring confidentiality for her clients. Therefore, no one could know the exact number of children in Tann's care, nor their whereabouts. By the late 1940s, complaints from adopting and birth parents resulted in an investigation of the Tennessee Children's Home Society.

Joan Crawford with Daughters Cathy and Cynthia,
Adopted from Georgia Tann

Georgia Tann died of cancer in September 1950, before any results of the investigation came to light. Judge Kelly resigned after twenty years on the bench and died in 1955. No one was ever prosecuted for the illegal adoptions. The Tennessee Children's Home Society was closed after Tann's death.

Some of Tann's more famous clients were soon in the spotlight. Joan Crawford had adopted children through Tann, as did June Allyson and Dick Powell. When the news about Tann's illegal operation broke in 1950, Crawford refused to comment, but Powell stated that the charges were "vicious political sniping."

In 1951, the State of Tennessee reviewed and revised adoption laws. Significantly a provision was made that all persons who had evidence they were adopted through the Tennessee Children's Home Society would be allowed access to all records concerning their case.

During her reign, it is estimated that Tann illegally placed more than 5,000 children. It may never be known how many infants died while in the 'care' of the Tennessee Children's Home Society but the number of children that died under the Tann's watch was so great that the infant mortality rate of Memphis was once the highest in the nation.

If you suspect that you or your family was affected by the unlawful acts of Georgia Tann and the Tennessee Children's Home Society, contact the State of Tennessee Department of Children's Services:

Department of Children's Services
Post Adoption Unit
Cordell Hull Building, 8ᵗʰ Floor
436 Sixth Avenue North
Nashville, TN 37243

* It is essential to note that the Tennessee Children's Home Society is not to be confused with the Tennessee Children's Home, which is accredited by the state of Tennessee. The Tennessee Children's Home has no connection with Georgia Tann or the Tennessee Children's Home Society.

Printed in Great Britain
by Amazon